IS LEGALISM A HERESY?

IS LEGALISM A HERESY?

Wayne G. Boulton

PAULIST PRESS
New York/Ramsey

The Publisher gratefully acknowledges the use of material from A Hidden Revolution *by Ellis Rivkin, copyright © 1978 by Ellis Rivkin, used by permission of Abingdon Press.*

Library of Congress
Catalog Card Number: 81-85386

ISBN: 0-8091-2431-9

Published by Paulist Press
545 Island Road, Ramsey, N.J. 07446

Printed and bound in the
United States of America

CONTENTS

TO
THE MEMORY OF
REINHOLD NIEBUHR
(1892-1971)

PREFACE

This book explores an ignored and often repressed dimension of Christ's universality. As defined in the New Testament, the universalism of Christianity is peculiar, for its even cosmic inclusiveness is coupled everywhere with a jarring narrowness at the center. This center is the man Jesus who, in a representative passage, refers to himself as "the way, the truth, and the life" (John 14:6). Each New Testament writer places Christ at the center of two concentric circles, the circle of the Church and the wider circle of all humanity. Because God's intent is to draw all mankind to himself through his Son (John 12), Christ's followers are instructed to expand the smaller circle and go the ends of the earth, making disciples in all nations (Matthew 28; Acts 1). In the terse formula of Paul, "one died for all" (2 Cor. 5:4).

Jesus is Christianity's universal person. But from the very beginning, different types of Christianity have described this universality in distinctive ways. Christians of the early Jerusalem church, or "Jewish Christians," sensed no boundary line between themselves and fellow Jews. They continued as faithful adherents to the law and stressed that Jesus had no wish to abandon it. The missionary Paul, who liberated the young faith from the tutelage of Judaism, was viewed as the arch-enemy, as the syncretistic culprit responsible for the rest of Christianity's rejection of the law. Jewish Christians came to prefer the Book of James to anything Paul or John ever wrote. In their vision, the risen Christ is portrayed as reaching out with particular sympathy and understanding toward the Jews.

Since the disappearance of Jewish Christianity in the fourth century A.D., the triumph of Hellenistic and Latin Christianity has been virtually complete. All anti-Judaic undertones in later Christian theology are conditioned by this fact. Until early in the twentieth century, Christian scholars had no idea that a peculiarly Jewish, legal form of orthodox Christianity ever existed. Its recovery promises to help Christians correct a one-sided theology that seems to lead inevitably to anti-Judaism.

1

Thanks to some recent research, this Jewish "theology of the losers" is now being reconstructed. The ethical position advocated in *Is Legalism A Heresy?* is inspired by a particular form of Judaism— the Pharisees, the villains of the New Testament. "The most significant distortion of ancient Judaism remaining in Christian consciousness," writes John Pawlikowski, is "the stereotyping of the Pharisees."[1] My thesis is that on a number of contemporary issues such as homosexuality (Ch. 7), the family (Ch. 6), violence and the state (Chs. 4–5), and responsible consumption (Ch. 8), the Pharisees represent a significant and neglected resource for Christian social ethics.

Most of the book was written on sabbatical at St. Mary's College in St. Andrews—a grey, haunted little university town on Scotland's east coast. I remain deeply grateful to the College Principal Jim Whyte and to Professor George Hall for their splendid hospitality and intellectual stimulation. Special thanks are due also to my wife, Vicki, a helpmeet in every sense of that beautiful, ancient word; to my two sons, Matt and Chris, who interrupted this project innumerable times, and gave me something better to do; to Father John Pawlikowski, for his early advice and assistance; to Hope College for its support in the form of two summer grants, but more for the quality of its faculty community; to colleagues Charles Huttar, Merold Westphal, Dave Myers, and to the entire religion department at Hope, for their perceptive and unfailingly constructive criticism; to Paulist Editor Larry Boadt, an ecumenical spirit of rare poise and patience; and to Marian Van Ry, a fine typist and a good friend.

Two chapters of this book appeared in shorter form as journal articles, and I am grateful to the editors of these journals for letting me use the material again. Parts of Chapter 4, "The Law of Government," appeared as "The Riddle of Romans 13" in the *Christian Century* (Sept. 15, 1976), pp. 758-761. Chapter 6, "The Law of the Family," is adapted from my "Patricia Hearst/Tania and a Theology of the Family," *Reformed Journal* (Sept. 1974), pp. 14-17.

A final acknowledgment is to my students. This book was born in the classroom, and is written by a college teacher. If you are an undergraduate and find Chapters 1 and 2 a little heavy, don't be discouraged. Most of the book is aimed at undergraduates, and I hope at least some of it challenges and provokes you. Students exactly like you helped to shape it.

NOTE

1. John T. Pawlikowski, *What Are They Saying about Christian-Jewish Relations?* (New York, 1980), p. 94.

INTRODUCTION

Two-thirds of what we see is behind our eyes.
Chinese Proverb

Though the intellectual origins of this book will doubtless be clearer to its critics than to its author, two deserve special mention. One is the man to whom the book is dedicated. Though I never met him, Reinhold Niebuhr has had a profound impact on me, as he did on many of his students. The depth of his impact became clear only as I began this study and discovered that many of its underlying themes—the respect for the Jewish tradition, the endorsement of political realism, the Anglophile fondness for social institutions that acknowledge law as the ultimate authority,[1] the affirmation of the Kantian tradition of ethical theology—all these bear the indelible Niebuhr stamp.

It was Niebuhr who first introduced me to the depth and complexity of the grace-law problem in Christian theology, and to the ways in which history is littered with premature solutions to it.[2] Perhaps my greatest indebtedness is to Niebuhr's own conception of the relation between love and law. In an essay first published in 1952, Niebuhr argued that "the dialectical relation of love to law . . . as fulfilling all possibilities of law and yet as standing in contradiction to it . . . is the basis and problem of all Catholic and Protestant speculations on the relation of love to law."[3] Throughout the remainder of the essay, Niebuhr's elaboration of the dialectic is brilliant and true. Though I emphasize law a good deal more than he ever did, my general approach to the subject is Niebuhrian.[4]

The other noteworthy source is Richard Rubenstein's 1966 essay on Harvey Cox's *The Secular City* (1965).[5] I can still remember the shock of reading this piece as a second year seminary student, and coming face to face with a brutal dissection of the provinciality, the materialism, the success orientation, and the anti-Jewish undercurrent in my own budding Protestant theology. I have yet to come

5

across a better brief analysis of liberal theology in the 1960's. And its author is a Jew.

But the essay did more than this. Like a flash of lightning on a dark night, it revealed instantly the ways in which the German death camps have changed the very landscape of Christian theology. This is particularly the case for the social gospel tradition of Cox's book and of liberation theology, a tradition which sees Christ's kingdom in the process of realizing itself within (usually Western) history. For scarcely forty years ago at the center of the Christian West, hell became flesh and dwelt among us; and over six million of those marked for death were Jews, while those who marked them called themselves Christians. Neither Jews nor Christians will ever be the same.

The holocaust reopens one of the oldest Jewish-Christian debates: What sense is there in the Christian claim that the Messiah has come? It leaves Rubenstein convinced that eschatology *per se* is an opiate, a sickness by means of which we conceal from ourselves our evil, failures and tragic fate as human beings. "Like the Pharisees of old," he writes, "I look in vain for any real evidence of God's redemptive work as continuously manifest in the world." The real significance of Pharisaism lies not in its compulsive attachment to a dead law, but rather in "its openness to the question of man's relation to God and fellowman in a world in which eschatological yearning is a vain and futile illusion." [6]

The book before you is not a "Christian response" to the holocaust. There may, in fact, be no such thing. Speaking in that gentle, searing voice which has instructed so many, Elie Wiesel is probably correct when he writes that those claiming "this or that" constitutes a response to the holocaust are content with very little.[7] Furthermore, I do not happen to agree with Rubenstein about post-holocaust eschatology. I don't completely agree with him about his Pharisees. But the questions he raises are so serious and so challenging to me that they provide an inescapable context for what follows.

I

At the heart of this book is a type of Christianity that on the surface resembles a variant of modern evangelicalism. But I call it "Pharisaic Christianity," claiming that its ethical origins are ancient, and may not lie quite where we think they do. Pharisaic Christianity is a form of Jewish Christianity. The purpose of the book is to explore selected subjects in political ethics from a Jewish Christian base.

The meaning of Jewish Christianity itself, however, is not self-evident. The term sometimes refers to the dependence of nearly all Christianity upon God's dealings with Israel. Here, though, Jewish Christianity means a *distinct type* of Christianity. Its theological position was first formulated in the Jerusalem circle dominated by James, a group which appears to have enjoyed considerable prestige in the early Church until the fall of Jerusalem in 70 A.D.[8] Some scholars contend that without Jewish Christian lobbying, Gentile Christianity would not have retained the Old Testament in the Christian canon.[9] If this is true, the historical importance of Jewish Christianity is difficult to overestimate. But detached from its native soil, the movement lost its vitality over the next three centuries, and gradually disappeared.

So Jewish Christianity is a type of *Christianity*. It is neither a third religion nor a magical formula in terms of which the tragic rupture between Christianity and Judaism can be overcome. The Hebrew Christian Jocz is probably right that this rupture is healed only in Christ-believing Jews themselves, and even there "not so much as the bridge from one to the other, but as the focus of the eschatological promise: All Israel shall be saved, (i.e.) . . . that God is still the God of Israel, of the Covenant, of the Promises."[10]

In terms of ethical theory, Jewish Christianity is law model Christianity. Jewish Christians stress the Jewishness of Jesus, and claim that he gave us no new ethics, for the Torah was already in place. What Jesus did, rather, was to extend, deepen and intensify the law, and to reveal in an unparalleled way the lawgiver to whom all are responsible.[11] Thus Jewish Christians can see and portray Christ as reaching out with sympathy and understanding toward other religions of the law model: toward Islam, toward the followers of Confucius, and particularly toward the Jews. But what exactly is this "law model"?

In 1963, H. Richard Niebuhr proposed that we are far more *symbolic* animals than rational ones. Visual and literary art in particular civilizations, Niebuhr argues, not only reflect the distinct ways that Egyptians or Greeks or Indians apprehend reality, but also guide the seeing itself. Symbol-making is essential to all human activity, not simply to religion and art, because even our language is a symbolic system. "Man as language-user, man as thinker, man as interpreter of nature, man as artist, man as worshipper, seems to be always symbolic man, metaphor-using, image-making, and image-using man."[12]

Niebuhr then applies this insight to the moral life, noting that we are every bit as dependent on images and metaphors in morality as elsewhere. Moral thought in the West proceeds for the most part from one of the three great symbolic forms or root-metaphors: we see ourselves either as makers, as responders, or as citizens. The mystery of the moral is such, he argues, that only an "old, though deeply established, prejudice" would lead us to conclude that one of these symbols alone is the right one.[13] Niebuhr stresses this by labeling each of the symbols "synecdoches," i.e., metaphors which apprehend and interpret all moral activity by making a *particular* activity representative of the whole. The distinguished ethicist might also have used Niels Bohr's principle of "complementarity" from contemporary physics. Why? Because all three approaches seek to give an account of the same thing—morality—through different frames of reference. The three frames tend to exclude each other, but also *complement* each other, so that only the juxtaposition of all of them provides a satisfactory theoretical (ethical) account of morality.

The first symbol, man as maker, is a dominant image in classical Greek thought, where everything in nature and history is defined according to its proper end or *telos*. In this model, the purpose of the moral life is to move individuals and communities toward the good, toward ideals. The most characteristic human activity is understood to be *making*, shaping as a craftsman the raw material of life according to a vision of its true end.[14]

A second grand symbol is responsibility, the metaphor Niebuhr himself prefers. It is the youngest of the three symbols, though hints of the response model can be found in Aristotle's notion of virtue as a mean betweens extremes, and in Stoicism and Taoism. This approach to morality begins with neither purposes nor law nor the individual self, but with responses and the self-in-relation. Man is understood as a responder, and the basic moral query is "What is going on?" The best action is the fitting action; it is that action most responsive to what is happening to us and to our interpretation of what is happening which "is alone conducive to the good and alone is right."[15]

The third symbol begins by asking not "What is my goal?" or "What is going on?" but "What is the law and what is the first law of my life?" This is the deontological or law model, where man is viewed as a citizen adhering to and rebelling against and creating laws or rules—of logic, of scientific method, of justice, and the like. Man is *homo politicus*. This is the dominant ethical metaphor in Hebrew thought; its champion in philosophy is Immanuel Kant.[16] It is in terms of this grand and ancient image that millions of Jews and Muslims view themselves and the world.

It is also precisely in terms of the law model that millions of *Christians* understand themselves and their world; and through them Christ reaches out to communities of the law in every nation and culture. This sort of Christianity and its ethics have a number of historical antecedents. One important precedent is Christian natural law. From early Stoic roots, the natural law tradition was Christianized and later received classical expression in the works both of Thomas Aquinas (1225-1274) and of the Elizabethan Richard Hooker (1553-1600). No less may be said of law, Hooker wrote, "than that her seat is the bosom of God, her voice the harmony of the world, all things in heaven and earth do her homage, the very least as feeling her care, and the greatest as not exempted from her power. . . ."[17]

Another historical source is the Anabaptist wing of the Reformation, with its rigorous focus on the New Testament portrait of Jesus as the "new law." But perhaps the most exemplary Christian tradition is Calvinism. It is not without reason that Calvinists are often criticized as "Judaizers" and "legalists." In sixteenth century Calvinist churches, and in these churches alone, the law (the Ten Commandments) was not only sung each Sunday by the congregation rather than read by the minister; its location in the worship service was changed to *follow* confession and absolution rather than precede them. This expressed Calvin's belief that for Christians the law becomes a joyful duty, the ethical dimension of proper praise (orthodoxy), the way of obedience to God.[18] The finest confessional elaboration of law model Christianity is probably the Calvinist Westminister Confession of 1645.

II

But the form of Christianity presented here is not called "Calvinist" or "Anabaptist" but "Pharisaic," which is to indicate that the original antecedent of *this* ethic lies outside the Christian tradition. The more Western Christians discover about other societies, minority communities, and ancient cultures, the more the promise in our twentieth century pluralism becomes mixed with pain, teaching once again the wisdom in humility and in an intellectual love for one's enemies.[19] The moment Christians begin to think systematically about morality, for example, they find themselves entering *ground already occupied,* and thus must at the outset give attention to the relation between New Testament ethics and other ethical systems. In our case, the ground happens to be occupied by the Pharisees. Note well that not one of H. Richard Niebuhr's root-metaphors for morality is exclusively Christian in origin.

The Hillelite Pharisees revolutionized the Jewish law tradition in three crucial respects. First, they taught that the law was actually "twofold," oral as well as written, and that to all individuals who obey it, God promises eternal life for the soul and resurrection for the body. Second, they intensified the social as well as the religious commandments, creating a form of inner constitutionalism among their adherents and prompting some intriguing ethical positions, such as pacifism. Third, the Pharisees insisted that obedience to God's complete law should not be practiced only in monastic seclusion or in a priestly class, for the temple was everywhere. The law claims all Jews wherever they live, and must be kept wherever they live. Thus the writen text of the Torah should continually be explained and applied to ordinary life situations not obtaining at the time of Moses.

Inspired by this model, Pharisaic Christianity is an account of the Christian faith that emphasizes its legal aspects when interpreting and applying it. The "Torah" or the canonical Scriptures here possess supreme legal authority as a *rule* of Christian faith and morals. The spirit of this sort of Christianity is summarized nicely in that "notorious" hymn to the law, Psalm 119.

Pharisaic Christianity contains a *contemporary political* ethic as well, and most of this book elaborates it. Its ideal typical features are identified in Chapter II. Pharisaic Christianity speaks to and within the tradition of Anglo-American constitutionalism.[20] Our age is one in which the religious foundations of constitutionalism have all but vanished. Yet the closer one gets to the ancient religious revolution among the Pharisees, the more apparent becomes its continuity with this modern political one.

At the heart of Western constitutionalism is a profound conviction about the sanctity of the person. Because every individual human being is of paramount worth, each member of the political community possesses a sphere of genuine autonomy. The constitutionalist preoccupation with the worth and dignity of the individual eventually gave rise to the notion of "rights" considered natural. The primary role of a constitution became defining and maintaining human rights against interference by the ruler (be that ruler a prince, a party, or a popular majority).[21] In sixteenth century Holland, seventeenth century England, and eighteenth century America, "liberty under law" was the revolutionary battle cry which produced, in each case, complex political structures designed to realize justice by protecting the individual and limiting tyranny.

Since the eighteenth century, the religious foundations of law, constitutions and freedom have become more obscure. The movement of revolution has shifted steadily in the direction of more collectivist ideals of fraternity (in the form of nationalism) and equality (in the form of socialism and communism), inclining toward an immanentist political religion which sees in revolution the dawn of a perfect society. In fact, the socialist politics of liberation theology is an outstanding example of Christians speaking to and within a contemporary political movement of substance. But this poses an intriguing question: Isn't a Christian affirmation of constitutionalism a throwback to the eighteenth century, politically passé, ignorant of the march of history and of possibilities unique to the 1980's?

The answer depends, of course, upon what these possibilities actually are. Predicting the future is not my game, but it appears to me that the belief in secular revolution is itself beginning to dissipate.

James Billington speculates that this "fire in the minds of men," which has legitimized so much authoritarianism in the twentieth century, may "dialectically prefigure some rediscovery of religious evolution to revalidate democracy in the twenty-first."[22] In a suggestive footnote, he points out that in 1979 alone, three signs of this "dialectic" appeared. Fundamentalist Islam dominated an unexpected revolution in Iran; some scholars see in today's charismatic and evangelical Christian movements the spearhead of a social revolution, a "second Protestant Reformation"; and the traditionalist Pope John Paul II began drawing mass crowds in many countries far in excess of those commanded by any political leaders.[23]

So legal Christianity, with its Jewish Christian base and constitutionalist ethos, may not be completely out of step with our time. This book explores a variety of ethical topics (Chapters III-VIII) from the standpoint of a "legalism" only apparently heretical. But I cheerfully admit that my friends here are the chief heavies of the New Testament, and it is to this "brood of vipers" (Matt. 23) that we now turn.

NOTES

1. See Dietrich Bonhoeffer's remarks on "the insurmountable and ultimate antimony" between Britain and Germany on this question. *Ethics,* Smith trans. (London, 1955), p. 240.

2. See particularly *The Nature and Destiny of Man,* Vol. II (New York, 1941, 1943, 1949), Chs. 1-7.

3. "Love and Law in Protestantism and Catholicism," *Christian Realism and Political Problems* (New York, 1953), pp. 141–42.

4. In most of his work, however, Niebuhr's relentless polemic against natural law, combined with his use of the shorthand phrase "the law of love," did less than justice to the subtlety of his position. See his concession to Paul Ramsey in Charles W. Kegley and Robert W. Bretall, eds., *Reinhold Niebuhr: His Religious, Social and Political Thought* (New York, 1956), pp. 434–36.

5. Reprinted in Richard L. Rubenstein, *After Auschwitz: Radical Theology and Contemporary Judaism* (New York, 1966), Ch. 11.

6. *Ibid.,* p. 193.

7. Elie Wiesel, "Recalling Swallowed-Up Worlds," *The Christian Century* (May 27, 1981), p. 612.

8. To so define the origins of Jewish Christianity is already to exclude numerous "Jewish Christian" groups of the first century A.D. that accepted Christ as a prophet or as a Messiah but not as the Son of God. The best known of these are the Ebionites, but included also are a wide variety of groups such as the disciples of Elkesai, among whom Gnostic dualism appears to have made its earliest appearance; and the politicized messianism of Cerinthus, a continuation of the Jewish nationalist movement with a Christian flavor. See Jean Daniélou, *The Theology of Jewish Christianity,* John Baker trans. (London, 1964), pp. 7–10, 64–69. Such a definition points beyond itself to the problem of identifying the *sort* of Judaism which makes Jewish Christianity Jewish. See below, Chapter I.

9. Jacób Jocz, *The Jewish People and Jesus Christ* (London, 1949), p. 198.

10. Jacób Jocz, *A Theology of Election* (London, 1958), p. 184.

11. In a perfect expression of this position, Carl F. H. Henry declares: "The moral law, as revealed in creation, in the Decalogue, in the discourses of Jesus, and in the criterion of the final judgment, is an organic unity.... Not even Christ can improve the moral law, for he is its ultimate source.... Instead of reversing it or revising it, Christ declares the whole law, including its least commandment, to be eternally binding. Hence he asserts the basic harmony and continuity of his ethic with the Old Testament ethic": *Christian Personal Ethics* (Grand Rapids, 1957), pp. 309–310.

12. H. Richard Niebuhr, *The Responsible Self* (New York, 1963), pp. 153–54.

13. *Ibid.,* p. 163. See below, Epilogue.

14. *Ibid.,* pp. 48–51.

15. *Ibid.,* p. 61.

16. *Ibid.,* pp. 51–54, 74. Edward L. Long, Jr. challenges Niebuhr's inclusion of Kant here, and for a telling reason. Though Kant's philosophical method is indeed deontological, his notion of authority is so formal and autonomous that his ethical thought is more appropriately termed deliberative than prescriptive or law-centered. *A Survey of Christian Ethics* (New York, 1967), p. 76.

17. Richard Hooker, *Of The Laws of Ecclesiastical Polity,* Book I, R. W. Church, ed. (Oxford, 1846), p. 106.

18. Howard Hageman, "The Law in the Liturgy," *God and the Good,* C. Orlebeke and L. Smedes, eds. (Grand Rapids, 1975), pp. 35–45.

19. See Donald W. Shriver, Jr., "The Promise and Pain of Pluralism," *The Christian Century* (March 27, 1980), pp. 345–50.

20. For a brief history, see Carl Friedrich, "Constitutions and Consti-

tutionalism," *International Encyclopedia of the Social Sciences,* Vol. III, David Sills, ed. (New York, 1968), pp. 318–326.

21. Carl J. Friedrich, *Transcendent Justice: Religious Dimensions of Constitutionalism* (Durham, N.C., 1964), pp. 15–20, 115. Note Friedrich's insistence (p. 17) that constitutionalism is a "continuing process," rather than simply a political order based upon a formal written document.

22. James Billington, *Fire in the Minds of Men: Origins of the Revolutionary Faith* (New York, 1980), p. 14.

23. *Ibid.,* p. 515. The scholars cited are Jeremy Rifkin and Thomas Howard in *The Emerging Order: God in the Age of Scarcity* (New York, 1979).

I

THE PHARISEES AND
THEIR TORAH

The law of the Lord is perfect,
   reviving the soul;
the testimony of the Lord is sure,
   making wise the simple;
the precepts of the Lord are right,
   rejoicing the heart;
the commandment of the Lord is pure,
   enlightening the eyes.

                              Psalm 19:7–8

Over one hundred years before the birth of Christ, the Pharisees emerged as a band of reformist Jewish teachers with some influence in Palestine. Despite vigorous opposition recorded in the Gospels, Jesus himself may have been one,[1] and the early Pharisaic training of the apostle Paul is well known. The mark of the Pharisees was their distinctive approach to divine Law and the claim that righteousness under the Law was the highest ideal. The extent and character of their influence is a disputed question in contemporary religious thought, primarily because the evidence is limited, often opaque and sometimes slanted. As a party with a self-conscious theological position, the Pharisees died out in the second century A.D.

But there is good reason to believe that the spirit of the Pharisees did not die. Pharisaism was the immediate ancestor of the rabbinic Judaism that followed the fall of Jerusalem; the authoritative corpus of Jewish oral law, the Mishnah, testifies to the Pharisees' enduring impact. Since only rabbinic Judaism survived antiquity, the

Pharisees are historically connected with medieval Judaism and the varied forms of contemporary Judaism as well. Matthew Black's notorious assertion that Pharisaism led to an "arid and sterile religion" is peculiar, coming as it does from such a distinguished and careful scholar, but even he admits a few lines later that the Pharisaic movement as a whole contains "important ideals and conceptions."[2]

The thesis of this book is that the distinctive ethos of the Pharisees lives on in the Christian community as well. And my purpose here is as much advocacy as analysis. I am not exactly neutral about this Pharasaic "legacy." So the thesis might better be stated thus: the Pharisaic spirit not only does but *should* live on in the Christian community. Most of what follows (Chs. 3–10) is one person's attempt to give Pharisaic Christianity contemporary, constructive expression. This first chapter examines the origins of the ethos, giving attention to its central and most significant element—Torah.

The Evidence and Neusner's Razor

"The history of Pharisaism," writes Professor Ellis Rivkin, "is largely non-recoverable because of the nature of the sources."[3] Quite so. There are three sources upon which scholars may legitimately draw to define and evaluate the Pharisees: Josephus, the Gospels, and the Talmudic traditions about the "rabbis." The four works of the Jewish historian Josephus—*The Jewish War, Antiquities, Life,* and *Against Arion*—were written in Rome between approximately 75 and 105 A.D., and are universally conceded to be the most important existing historical works on the Jews in antiquity. His references to the Pharisees are not extensive, and occur primarily in stories about them as a political party operating in the time of the Maccabees, from about 160–60 B.C. In the *Antiquities,* a history of Israel down to 70 A.D., we are told that the Pharisees were so popular that no government hoping to rule Palestine could do without their support. But in his first book, *The Jewish War,* no such claim is made. They appear simply as a party active in the Maccabean court, and hold two distinct doctrines—a view of divine providence consistent with human freedom, and human survival after death.[4]

The Gospels contain a variety of stories and sayings about the Pharisees. They were shaped by about 80 A.D., and are dominated by accounts of Jesus' virulent attack on the Pharisees as "hypocrites," "blind fools," and a "brood of vipers."[5] But the portrait of the Pharisees in the New Testament is not uniformly negative. In the Luke-Acts tradition, references to an alliance between early followers of Jesus and the Pharisees are quite explicit. In Luke 13, some Pharisees warn Jesus that Herod wants to kill him. In Acts 5, the Pharisee Gamaliel defends Peter and other disciples before the high priest and his council, saving the defendants from almost certain death. In Acts 23 and 26, Paul stresses the proximity between the Pharisaic belief in resurrection and his own belief.

The rabbinic traditions about the Pharisees constitute the largest single source of information, and the most difficult to exploit. They occur in documents edited between about 200 A.D. and 600 A.D., and contain material likely to have been transmitted orally for *centuries*. Law and lore abound, with virtually no discernible historical sequence. One definition of the Pharisees emerging from the literature is a table-fellowship concerned with ritual purity and dietary laws.[6]

Only these rabbinic traditions, the Gospels, and the writings of Josephus derive from a time when the Pharisees flourished, and mention them by name. And the evidence, to understate a little, is not as coherent as we might like. Moreover, the question of the Pharisees is often a most sensitive issue in theological disputes between Christians and Jews, a factor which usually impedes objective investigation. The situation could hardly be otherwise: Jews begin with the Pharisees as beloved ancestors, attested in the Mishnah; Christians begin with a negative picture of them firmly embedded in the New Testament. So both religious communities should be grateful for the recent work of two outstanding scholars of the Pharisees. Both men have mastered the key sources, and have spent much of their lives investigating and writing about this controversial group. They are Ellis Rivkin and Jacob Neusner.

Professor Rivkin has been refining his thesis about the Pharisees for over thirty years, and recently published his conclusions in *A Hidden Revolution* (1978).[7] In this ground-breaking book, the Pharisees emerge as among the most daring innovators in Western history. Their central doctrine was a sort of inner constitutionalism, based at once on an audacious absorption into Judaism of Greco-Roman

modes of thinking and Greco-Roman institutions, and on the Pharisees' distinctive view that God holds out for the law-abiding individual eternal life for the soul and resurrection for the body. The
content of this inner constitution was the famous "twofold Law,"
i.e., the written and the oral, which was the main item in dispute between the Pharisees and their great enemies, the Sadducees.

The genius of Rivkin's Pharisees turns out to be political as well
as religious. The immediate effect of Pharisaic belief on the individual, he argues, was to intensify Jewish Law, making it internally
more binding than ever. For example, when an Athenian citizen left
ancient Athens, Athenian law ceased to be the Law for him. But for
Pharisaic Jews, the Law—the inner constitution—went wherever
they went. Their political master stroke was to use this doctrine to
sharply reduce the established power and influence of the priesthood
(read: Sadducees) and to gain widespread support from Jews of the
time, democratizing and virtually transforming Judaism in the process. In addition, Rivkin claims that they provided much of the bed-
rock for Christianity.[8]

But if the revolution is this old and this fundamental, why have
we taken so long to discover it? Rivkin's book suggests many reasons. First, as we have seen, the sources are tricky, and demand a
sophisticated, sensitive eye with access to the original material. Second, the historical documents assume the revolution rather than explain it. Third, the Pharisees themselves did not acknowledge what
they were doing. Finally, in a passage truly moving and clear, Rivkin
writes that even he would not have seen the Pharisaic revolution had
he not experienced their life.

It was because I lived the life of the twofold Law, believed
in the God of the twofold Law, hoped for eternal life, and
dreaded eternal punishment that I could discover *A Hidden
Revolution.* Whereas other scholars, Jewish and Christian,
list the belief in resurrection as a Pharisaic tenet, they do
not convey what the belief in resurrection means to an individual who believes literally that God will raise the dead.
These scholars do not communicate what such good news
must have meant to Jews nurtured on the Pentateuchal

proclamation that rewards and punishments are to be meted out in this world only. . . . The notion of *A Hidden Revolution* was thus seeded by my early life in Judaism. . . . When . . . I gained access to the tools of modern critical scholarship, I used these tools to reveal that the primordial power of Pharisaism lay in its proclamation that God so loved the individual that he revealed to Israel a twofold Law which, if internalized and obeyed, would lead to eternal life for the soul and resurrection for the body. It was this triadic teaching that so stirred the Jews that they abandoned the literal, written Pentateuch for a Law that had never been written down. It was this triadic teaching that stirred Paul to substitute Christ for the twofold Law. It was this triadic teaching that almost two thousand years later gave my family the strength to follow the twofold Law, whatever the sacrifice and however demanding the discipline. It was this triadic teaching on which I was nurtured and upon which I still look back with such reverent awe.[9]

Rivkin's book is a stunning reconstruction of the Pharisees from the key sources, and should remain a standard work for years to come.

The characteristics of Neusner's studies of the Pharisees, on the other hand, are extraordinary thoroughness combined with icy historical skepticism with respect to the sources. In 1971, he published a massive, three-volume translation and analysis of rabbinic traditions about the Pharisees before 70 A.D., and followed it with a summary of his position in Pharisaic studies, *From Politics to Piety: The Emergence of Pharisaic Judaism* (1973). For Neusner, the most serious inadequacy in Jewish and Christian studies of the Pharisees is an *historical* one.

It appears, typically, in two forms. In Neusner's judgment, a depressingly large number of Pharisaic studies are based on a false conception of the evidence, claiming in one way or another that a particular story contains an exact historical record of what actually happened. He follows Rudolf Bultmann in criticizing Christians for assuming this about materials in the New Testament, and he criticizes anyone when it is assumed about other sources, particularly the

rabbinic traditions. The second mistake, often combined with the
first, is an error in historical generalization—the tendency to say far
more than all the data together permit.

> We commonly find a source cited without attention to how
> it is supposed to prove the "fact" it purportedly contains.
> Systematic and disciplined analysis of texts is rare, allu-
> sions to unexamined texts commonplace. . . . The fault lies
> in the false presumption that nearly all sources, appearing
> in any sort of document, early, late, or medieval, contain
> accurate historical information about the men and events
> of which they speak.[10]

Neusner's formidable command of the original sources in Pharisaic studies, plus his disciplined skepticism with respect to their historical reliability, gives him a critical slant and tool that might be
called Neusner's "razor." His current prominence in the field is due
in no small measure to the effectiveness with which he wields it.
Most important for our purposes is his telling critique of Christian
biblical scholarship on the Pharisee question under the heading
"Theology in Historical Guise."[11]

Rudolf Bultmann will serve as a representative example. To
Bultmann's use of literary-critical and historical-critical methods to
analyze ancient sacred texts, Neusner has no objection. In fact, he
commends *The History of the Synoptic Traditions,*[12] except to claim
in passing that Bultmann's knowledge of rabbinic traditions is based
entirely on secondary sources.[13] But when Bultmann uses his own
theology to help him move from the evidence to historical generalization, Neusner goes after him, and for good reason.

He calls Bultmann's *Primitive Christianity in Its Contemporary
Setting* (1965) "apologetics of a rather crude sort" and "theology in
the past tense of a historical essay." Why? Not so much because
Bultmann is demonstrably wrong, as because the available data is
such as to make it impossible to show whether he is right or wrong!
In *Primitive Christianity* Bultmann asserts that Pharisaic Judaism
"cut herself off from the outside world and lived in extraordinary
isolation" (p. 60). Interpretation of the Holy Scriptures in the community was "primitive and, despite certain variations, stereotype . . .

there was no attempt to reach a deeper understanding of the context, to discover the ideas underlying the text itself" (p. 64). Religious life was legalistic and formal, because "radical obedience would have involved a personal assent to divine command, whereas in Judaism so many of the precepts were trivial or unintelligible that the kind of obedience produced was formal rather than radical" (p. 68).

This, argues Neusner, is opinion masquerading as historical fact. The data on which these statements might be based does not exist. In Neusner's words, Bultmann "simply does not know what he is talking about."

> My criticism is not that Bultmann is ignorant of rabbinical traditions about the Pharisees, but that he makes statements which cannot be founded upon any evidence now available or likely to become available. It is as if, like other scholars, he accused the Pharisees of being "hypocrites" or "the brood of Satan." Without knowledge of their true feelings, shown, for instance, by diaries or personal interviews, how are we to know whether the Pharisees were, or were not, characterized by hypocrisy.... A work on historical problems, moreover, cannot rightly introduce considerations irrelevant to the historical inquiry. "Radical Obedience" may be a fruitful theological category, but helps not at all to understand the nature of life under the law.[14]

Neusner is not to be followed slavishly, of course; he has his peculiar sympathies. But his "razor" is salutary for all who would proceed responsibly on the question of the Pharisees. This is so precisely because the evidence does prompt such varied interpretations, some of which have proved all too useful in the service of a Christian theology patently designed to proclaim the Messiah by negating the Jews.[15]

The essence of the matter is that though theology and history can and should influence each other, they are *different* disciplines. The boundary between them must be watched carefully. The Law-Gospel dichotomy, for example, is a time-honored distinction in Christian theology. But Professor Kirster Stendahl is surely right that the distinction has proved to be itself a most powerful form of anti-Judaism. "According to this model," he writes, "Jewish attitudes and Jewish piety are by definition the sample of the wrong attitudes toward God."[16] Just so. We should be wary of all such apparently innocuous categories, and instead ask of each text on the Pharisees: What sort of evidence is this? What generalizations may properly be based upon it?

The Law-Centered Ethos of the Pharisees

Approached with appropriate care, then, what exactly do the Pharisee documents tell us? Each interpreter must make crucial choices here, and mine fill the remainder of this chapter. E. P. Sanders' superb book, *Paul and Palestinian Judaism* (1977),[17] has at least two important bearings on my position. The first is his concentration on meaningful pattern or ethos in religion, i.e., his structuralism. Sanders effectively argues that to understand any part(s) of early Judaism (prayer, ritual washing, etc.), one must define the essential pattern of religion in which this part(s) is perceived by its adherents to function. This essential pattern in any religion, he writes, is how adherents understand getting into it and staying in it.[18] Sanders' methodological position, then, is that knowledge of this whole is a *sine qua non* for understanding the parts.

Secondly and partly as a result of his methodological insight, Sanders overturns the view, widespread in New Testament scholarship, that first century Judaism degenerated into a religion of legalistic works-righteousness, a religion in which salvation had always to be earned and could thus never be certain. This position that so many have learned to hold rests, Sanders claims, on a prior commitment to Christianity (for which Judaism becomes a convenient foil) and on the work of scholars with no primary command of the rabbinic literature. Based on just such command, Sanders' attack is magisterial and devastating.[19]

He calls the law-centered structure of Palestinian Judaism "covenantal nomism," and I concur with his hypothesis that this basic ethos must have pervaded all forms of the Judaism encountered by Jesus and Paul, including the Pharisees.[20] The pattern begins with and presupposes the election of Israel and the covenant relation with

God. The stress on obedience to Law ("nomism"), therefore, is a matter of response to the salvation already provided by the mercy of God, and not an attempt to compile merit before a distant deity to win his favor.

The ethos of covenantal nomism is conveniently summarized by Sanders as follows:

> (1) God has chosen Israel and (2) given the law. The law implies both (3) God's promise to maintain the election and (4) the requirement to obey. (5) God rewards obedience and punishes transgression. (6) The law provides for means of atonement, and atonement results in (7) maintenance or re-establishment of the covenantal relationship. (8) All those who are maintained in the covenant by obedience, atonement and God's mercy belong to the group which will be saved.[21]

In such an ethos, there is clearly no *necessary* tendency toward legalism, though it is not only possible but likely that some adherents would so tend.[22] In classical Christian ethics, the essence of legalism is its Pelagian assumption that salvation can be procured through human effort, in this case through works of obedience. It is exactly this perversion of nomism that is undercut by the covenant, central in Old Testament theology, wherein election and ultimately salvation are considered to be by God's mercy and not by human achievement. In this system, obedience is a condition of *remaining* righteous; it does not and cannot elect, it does not and cannot save, it does not and cannot earn God's grace as such.

The outstanding feature of the covenantal nomism unique to the Pharisees is their expansion of the Torah. Torah means teaching: it does not merely mean laws. "Unless that elementary fact be clearly grasped and constantly borne in mind," writes Travers Herford, "there is no possibility of understanding Pharisaism."[23] Though itself a common Hebrew word denoting any kind of teaching, Torah had acquired by the time of Ezra a specific religious meaning—the teaching which God had given through Moses for the guidance and instruction of Israel. The Torah of Moses was to become the supreme authority in Israel, the guide of its actions and the source of its knowledge of divine will. It was *written* in the five books attributed to Moses that formed the Pentateuch.

In the Torah, God required that all his people be holy if they are to be his people, and it enjoined separation from uncleanness and from whatever the Torah defined as imparting impurity. Most Jews believed this. *But how was this separation to be achieved?* The Pharisees and their expanded, "twofold" Torah emerged out of a debate over this question.

The Pharisees concluded that everyone should be in a state of ritual purity. All of Israel must separate herself from the world. But this was to be achieved not in geographical isolation on the shores of the Dead Sea, or within the Temple. The proper enclave in which Jewish people could present themselves holy before God was within the Torah itself, no matter where they lived. To keep the Law where they lived, however, people must know what the Torah *means:* its definitions must be made intelligible and applicable to situations not obtaining in the time of Moses. Hence the Pharisees expanded the educational role of the synagogue, gave extreme attention to interpreting and applying the written text of the Torah to new circumstances, and came to believe that the "oral law" (traditions of interpretation) was as important as the written.[24]

Thus the Law for the Pharisees was in a peculiar sense *alive.* The Pharisaic pattern suggests nicely that the *living* God was the author of this Law, and that he is active in its growth, interpretation, and application, as well as concerned about its actual effect. This is not an unhistorical, static concept of law. Indeed, as Neusner has stressed, an outstanding feature of the Pharisees was their historical responsiveness, especially to the destruction of the Temple in 70 A.D. Accepting powerlessness, they moved "from politics to piety," reshaping the life of Jewry in a way appropriate to the new situation. They abandoned politics and yet at the same time concentrated on what they believed was essential to politics: building a sacred community, fulfilling all the laws of the Torah.[25]

In the Pharisaic view of history, then, one can detect a marked resistance to the politicization of Jewish messianism.[26] To be sure, we should reject the contention that apocalyptic Judaism—with its heightened expectation of an imminent end—and Pharisaic "legalistic" Judaism were substantially different religious types.[27] The evidence suggests, rather, that one was quite as covenantal and as nomistic as the other. However, there does appear to have been a tension between them. In the Hillelite texts, for example, in a time and place when messianism was a burning issue, not a single reference to the messianic idea appears.[28]

Why? Since the Pharisees believed in the resurrection and in the coming of the Messiah, the answer may lie in the way certain of their enemies interpreted these beliefs. Herford explains it by pointing to the ease with which apocalyptic literature can be mixed with the spirit of national pride and vindictive hatred, fueling the passions of war. In a time of widespread persecution and oppression, there may have been a practical alliance betwen apocalyptic ideas and the party of the Zealots. The Pharisees were bound to distance themselves from writings which inflamed the zeal of those most critical of the Pharisaic policy of peaceful co-existence. But Herford also offers another, perhaps more profound explanation. At the heart of Pharisaism was an austere hope in the many finite, fallible human means of following God in establishing his Kingdom on earth. Apocalypticism, on the other hand, was often despair parading as hope—a distrust of the slow waiting for God's purpose to be fulfilled, a rejection of his revealed command to serve him in the present. It may well have been this despair that the Pharisees opposed when they opposed politicized messianism.[29]

The Hillel School and Jesus

Josephus and the rabbinic traditions attest to many tensions and divisions within the first century Judaism. The Romans' initial perception of Christianity—as yet another Jewish sect—was perfectly logical given the circumstances. There were serious differences between the monastic Teachers of Righteousness (Essenes), the priestly Sadducees, the Pharisees, and the Zealots. But there was also conflict within the Pharisaic party itself. In Jesus' time, the most important of these divisions appears to have been between the House of Hillel and the House of Shammai.

Hillel the Elder, perhaps the greatest Pharisaic leader, lived from about 50 B.C. to 10 A.D. His name dominates all the rabbinic traditions about the Pharisees. Many sayings attributed to him are quite similar, even in the exact wording, to the teachings of Jesus.[30]

The Pharisaic Shammaites, on the other hand, were said to display greater strictness and more propensity to violence than the disciples of Hillel. If the bellicose Zealots were indeed an offshoot of the Pharisees (their "wild men"), they were almost certainly closer to the Shammai school than to Hillel.[31] After carefully sifting through Shammaite teaching, Asher Finkel concludes that Jesus' harsh "woes" against the Pharisees may have been directed entirely at the zealous disciples of Shammai's academy.[32]

Focusing on the Hillel school alone, one can note three characteristics that veer remarkably close to what we know of the first followers of Jesus.

1. *Puritanism.* This, after all, is what the Pharisees are known for: an overriding passion for holiness, for ritual and ethical purity. With the Essenic communities, they saw their first job as attacking theological and ethical laxity *inside* the camp.[33] In the Hebrew sources, they are called *perushim,* or "separatists." They were called out ("elected") from the rest of society to purify themselves before a holy and righteous God, i.e., to follow him and do his will.

The mechanism for implementing this puritanism, as Rivkin shows, was *intensification of the whole Law,* i.e., of the religious and the social commandments. It is important not to confuse this legal intensification among the Pharisees with more modern forms of ethical rigorism, such as intentionalism or formalism. No evidence I have seen suggests that their intensification entailed replacing the Law's traditional focus on behavior with a focus on intent, though it definitely is *extended* to intent or the "inner man." Nor do they attempt to universalize the Law by evacuating its content, as for example in Kant's categorical imperative. It is precisely the *content* of the Law that the Pharisees intensified, and their moral purpose appears to have been—as Professor G. Barbour once wrote in another connection—to manifest goodness "at so high a power that it pierces through all conventions and prejudices to that faculty of moral perception and response which is the most fundamental thing in human nature."[34] In Jewish terms, the Law intensified is still *halakah* for the Pharisees; i.e., its focus remains the way to live according to the commandments, not stories about God or theological principles (*hagga-dah*).[35]

A similar intensification of the Law is evident in parts of the New Testament, particularly in the synoptic tradition, where followers of Jesus are expected to give up home (Mark 10:8ff), family (Luke 14:26), possessions (Mark 10:17ff), and protection (Matthew 5:38f). The puritanism in the Sermon on the Mount is clear: Seek the Kingdom of God first (Matthew 6:33). That is to say, all other political, financial, domestic obligations come *second*.

2. *Egalitarian Realism.* The Sadducees and the Essenes, of course, were also puritanical in the above sense. But the Essenes abruptly left society and construed God's claim as a call to monastic perfectionism—after which they would clobber the Romans.[36] The Sadducees restricted the scope of God's claim to a priestly class. The Pharisees rejected both options, extending purity requirements to the laity (the Temple should be everywhere) and adapting the Law to normal everyday life.

The Pharisaic insistence that everyone should be a priest and that the written Law should be adapted to ordinary life by the unwritten law[37]—this dual contention could be called their egalitarian realism. It is the accommodationism of the Pharisees that made them vulnerable to the charge of hypocrisy, for they were attempting to do two contradictory things: intensify the commandments, and adapt them to everyday life. Such a charge is perhaps inevitable, particularly from an outsider's point of view.

Yet a similar form of accommodation can be detected among the first followers of Jesus. A glance at early Christian commentary on the famous Rich Young Ruler story (Mark 10:17–22) may provide evidence enough.[38] If not, how else should one construe the *range* of teachings on divorce in the New Testament—from its prohibition in Mark 10 to the "exceptive phrase" in Matthew 19 to the "Pauline privilege" in 1 Corinthians 7, etc.?

3. *Pacifism.* The most striking ethical characteristic shared by Hillelite Pharisees and the first followers of Jesus was their pacifism. They were the two peace parties among renewal movements within Judaism, a factor which emerges in bold relief when compared with

their environment. Revolt against brutal Roman suppression was endorsed by the Zealots and the Essenes; both groups demanded hatred
of foreigners.[39] The disciples of Shammai were notoriously aggressive
in enforcing their master's decision. Rabbinic sources attest that they
threatened and killed some teachers who opposed them.[40]

In contrast, the reduction of aggression in Hillelite and early
Christian circles was unmistakable. Hillel's policy toward the Shammaites was peaceful co-existence. An emphasis on leniency, restraint,
and particularly on humility permeates his teachings.[41] Similarly, Jesus and early Christians sharply condemned the murder of Zechari-
ah which was arranged by resistance fighters (Matthew 23:35).
Foreign soldiers are seen in a positive light (Matthew 8:5ff). Both a
zealot and a tax collector for the Romans are included in the most
intimate group of disciples (Matthew 10:3; Luke 6:15).[42]

These points of similarity between Hillelite Pharisaism and
Christianity—puritanism, egalitarian realism, and pacifism—are all
based on the available evidence. Neusner's warning should not be
forgotten, however. The historical reliability of much of the evidence
is, at best, difficult to judge. The conclusions suggested here are
drawn from the evidence, rather than demonstrated by it. Particularly with the Pharisees, two-thirds of what we see is behind our eyes.

In sum, the Pharisees are a long-neglected resource for contemporary Christian political ethics. Their position revolves around a
distinctive, dynamic view of law. The Pharisaic revolution parallels
that dramatic extension of the concept of law in Roman and Greek
jurisprudence, an expansion which successfully challenged the popular identification of law and command, and eventually became
known as "natural law" (*ius naturale*).

At the end of his history of natural law, A. P. d'Entrèves makes
a cogent appeal to anyone interested in ethics, and then slips:

> If he [the moralist] be a man of the *verum,* he will not ig-
> nore that the certainty for which conscience craves is not
> that of transient laws, but that of absolute values. He will
> provide such grounds for obedience as are capable of carry-
> ing conviction. But he will also take into account the unre-

lenting quest of man to rise above the "letter of the law" to the realm of the spirit. He will draw the dividing line between mere conformity to the law and the real value of action, between the Pharisee and the truly moral man.[43]

It is about time that scholarly and religious communities put such references to the Pharisees firmly and permanently behind them. We now know that d'Entrèves' last eight words are nothing more or less than an academic anachronism; Neusner's razor cuts them to ribbons. If the evidence suggests anything, it is the conclusion of this chapter: the Pharisee *was* a truly moral man.

NOTES

1. So argues William F. Phipps in "Jesus, the Prophetic Pharisee," *Journal of Ecumenical Studies,* Vol. 14, No. 1 (Winter, 1977), pp. 17–31. See also J. Klausner, *Jesus of Nazareth,* Mosh, tr. (New York, 1926).

2. Matthew Black, "Pharisees," *Interpreter's Dictionary of the Bible,* George A. Buttrick, *et al.,* eds. (New York & Nashville, 1962), III, p. 781. Jacob Neusner's dismissal of Black's choice of language as "the sort of anti-Judaism which has nothing to do with either historical facts or lack of historical facts," and as "familiar in the anti-Semitic writings of every age" is harsh, but difficult to refute: *The Rabbinic Traditions about the Pharisees Before 70* (Leiden, 1971), III, p. 362.

3. Ellis Rivkin, "Pharisaism and the Crisis of the Individual in the Greco-Roman World," *Jewish Quarterly Review,* 61 (1970), p. 31.

4. Josephus, *Antiquities,* L. Feldman, tr. (Cambridge, 1965), pp. 9–13; *War,* trans. H. St. J. Thackeray (Cambridge, 1956), pp. 385–87.

5. Matthew 23:13, 17, 33. See below, Chapter 9.

6. This is Jacob Neusner's judgment in *From Politics to Piety: The Emergence of Pharisaic Judaism* (Englewood Cliffs, 1973), Chapter 5.

7. Ellis Rivkin, *A Hidden Revolution: The Pharisees' Search for the Kingdom Within* (Nashville, 1978).

8. *Ibid.,* pp. 296–311.

9. *Ibid.,* pp. 22–24.

10. Neusner, *From Politics to Piety,* p. 6. See also his *Rabbinic Traditions,* III, pp. 320–23.

11. Neusner, *Rabbinic Traditions,* III, p. 359. He could have said a *certain sort* of theology in historical guise.

12. Rudolf Bultmann, *The History of the Synoptic Tradition,* J. Marsh, tr. (Oxford, 1963).

13. Neusner, *Rabbinic Traditions,* III, pp. 78–88.

14. *Ibid.,* p. 363.

15. This is not the opinion of Jews alone, of course. Nor is it a problem about which the Christian theological community has, to any significant degree, "come of age." See Sr. Charlotte Klein, *Anti-Judaism in Christian Theology,* E. Quinn, tr. (London, 1978).

16. Krister Stendahl, "Judaism and Christianity: A Plea for a New Relationship," *Cross Currents,* 17 (Fall 1967), p. 450. Many otherwise fair studies of the Pharisees are flawed by an uncritical use of the distinction. For example, see Hugo Odeberg, *Pharisaism and Christianity,* Moe, tr. (Concordia, 1964).

17. E. P. Sanders, *Paul and Palestinian Judaism* (London, 1977).

18. *Ibid.,* p. 17.

19. *Ibid.,* pp. 33–233.

20. *Ibid.,* p. 426.

21. *Ibid.,* p. 422.

22. See below, Chapter 9.

23. Travers Herford, *The Pharisees* (London, 1924), p. 54.

24. John Bowker, *Jesus and the Pharisees* (London, 1973), pp. 15–17.

25. Neusner, *From Politics to Piety,* pp. 143–54. The political strategy here appears Platonic: founding politics on ethics through education. Plato could commend this in *The Republic* because he believed, as did the Pharisees, that the principle of action which guides society and the state is the same as that which guides the individual. See Werner Jaeger, *Paideia* (New York, 1943), II, pp. 365–66.

26. Samuel Umen, *Pharisaism and Jesus* (New York, 1963).

27. Sanders, *Paul and Palestinian Judaism,* p. 423.

28. Nathan Glatzer, "Hillel the Elder in Light of the Dead Sea Scrolls," *The Scrolls and the New Testament,* Krister Stendahl, ed. (London, 1958), p. 242.

29. Herford, *The Pharisees,* pp. 186–93. He cites the mournful book of IV Ezra, written soon after the fall of Jerusalem in the first war, as clear evidence of the close connection between Apocalyptic and despair.

30. However, see Neusner, *From Politics to Piety,* pp. 41–44, where he rightly warns against overestimating the historical reliability of rabbinic traditions about Hillel.

31. Klausner, *Jesus of Nazareth,* pp. 204ff.

32. Asher Finkel, *The Pharisees and the Teacher of Nazareth* (Leiden, 1964), pp. 129–43.

33. For a comparison of what the rabbinic traditions attribute to Hillel and the Dead Sea Scrolls say about the Essene order, see Nathan Glatzer, "Hillel the Elder in Light of the Dead Sea Scrolls," pp. 232–44.

34. G. F. Barbour, *A Philosophical Study of Christian Ethics* (London, 1911), p. 299. Cf. Psalm 119:134.

35. My opinion is that Judaism as a whole is essentially halakic (primarily concerned with the way to live—from *halak*, "to walk"), though some Jewish scholars hold a different view. For a useful summary of the issue, see W. D. Davies, *The Gospel and the Land* (Berkeley, 1974), pp. 390–404.

36. Finkel, *The Pharisees and the Teacher of Nazareth,* p. 129.

37. Neusner, *From Politics to Piety,* pp. 151–52.

38. See John Passmore's skeptical and generally sound account of Christian perfectibilism based on this passage, in *The Perfectibility of Man* (New York, 1970), pp. 116–33.

39. Rule of the Community, 1.10. Quoted in Gerd Theissen, *The First Followers of Jesus,* Bowden, tr. (London, 1978), p. 64.

40. Finkel, *The Pharisees and the Teacher of Nazareth,* pp. 136, 142.

41. *Ibid.,* pp. 134, 143.

42. The saying that Jesus does not bring peace, but a sword (Luke 12:51–53), clearly refers to familial rather than military conflict. See below, Chapters 5 and 6.

43. A. P. d'Entrèves, *Natural Law* (New York, 1965), p. 121.

II

PHARISAIC CHRISTIANITY

> Think not that I have come to abolish the law and the proph-
> ets; I have come not to abolish them but to fulfill them. For
> truly, I say to you, till heaven and earth pass away, not an
> iota, not a dot, will pass from the law until all is accom-
> plished. Whoever then relaxes one of the least of these com-
> mandments and teaches men so, shall be called least in the
> kingdom of heaven; but he who does them and teaches them
> shall be called great in the kingdom of heaven. For I tell you,
> unless your righteousness far exceeds that of the scribes and
> Pharisees, you will never enter the kingdom of heaven.
>
> Matthew 5:17–20

Just as there appears to have been considerable variety *within*
the Jewish Christian sector of the early church,[1] so there is variety
among Pharisaic Christians today. The heart of this book, Chapters
3–8, is simply one version of Pharisaic Christianity focused on political ethics. Nonetheless, though the content varies, there are certain
structural characteristics common to all versions. These are the view
of the Bible in Pharisaic Christianity, its theological temper, its out-
look on ethics, its political position, and its ecclesiology. Of these
five, by far the most important is the first.

1. View of Scripture: The Bible as Torah

In Pharisaic Christianity, the written words of the Old and New
Testaments possess supreme authority as a rule of faith and morals.
This feature alone gives un undeniably Protestant cast to the posi-

tion. Indeed, the Pharisaic Christian ethos stands deeply in debt to that aggressive recovery of biblical authority among European Protestant theologians in this century—especially in the work of Karl Barth, Emil Brunner, and Dietrich Bonhoeffer. It agrees with Brevard Childs' contention that the basic locus of biblical authority is Scripture as a whole or the canon.[2] The Torah is not only in the canon; it is the canon. In Pharisaic Christianity, then, the authority of Scripture is like that of a written constitution. The best church order, to paraphrase Plato, would logically be one in which the Torah rules the rulers.

So Scripture as a whole is believed to be inspired by God. But are the words of the Torah identical to the words of God? At the one extreme, Christian fundamentalists like Harold Lindsell believe that they are.[3] At the other, Jack Sanders recommends that Christians select out of the Bible only those concepts that modern people can accept.[4] With perhaps the majority of the Jews and Christians, the position of Pharisaic Christianity is between these two extremes: while the words of the Torah are from God and inspired by God, they also have a quite human origin. The communion between the divine word and human words in Scripture is such that they can never be divided or separated, but also they should never be confused or identified.

If Scripture is *Torah,* what exactly is that? The formal meaning of Torah to Pharisaic Christians is much the same as its meaning throughout Judaism for 2,500 years. To call Scripture Torah is to claim that it is God's revelation of his gracious way with his people, and of how his people should live. As noted in Chapter 1, the word has a much wider range than "law," the English term often considered its equivalent. As Norman Lamm writes, Torah should never be reduced to its "nomos" elements, but includes many types of spiritual edification such as parables, sagas, songs, and the like.[5]

Put another way, Scripture as Torah is a formal feature of the "covenantal nomism" (Sanders) of Pharisaic Christianity. From Genesis to Revelation, biblical imperatives are an integral part of God's gracious covenant with his people. They are both instruments of grace and a complement to grace, which is why the unlinking of command and covenant is usually so crippling and often disastrous. It would be a surprise, incidentally, if some early Christians didn't accuse Jews of doing exactly this—for they continued to follow the commandments, but didn't recognize the God of grace in Jesus. Therefore: they in fact mustn't be following the commandments.

To be sure, covenantal nomism is still nomism. The imperative dimension of the Torah is its most visible element, an essential instrument in God's gracious leading among his people. But it is not the sum of grace. Divine mercy goes beyond divine justice. One of the classical functions of biblical commandments themselves, in fact, is to convince the faithful that one cannot live by commandments alone, but only by divine mercy and forgiveness. The moral law in Scripture reveals at once God's righteousness and human self-righteousness and self-deception, prompting us to seek God's help. Calvinists and Lutherans call this the first or "convicting" use of the law.[6] From a Pharisaic perspective, legalism can be succinctly defined as the evasion of law—in its first use.

Scripture requires continual interpretation and application. Thus while the Bible is the supreme authority in Pharisaic Christianity, it is not the only one. Authority is also invested in those leaders, identified by the faithful community, who interpret Scripture. For to faith, this book is ever adaptable to each generation because it contains the living word of God. This is why the message and meaning of Scripture is necessarily opaque apart from the community God is calling to faith. As Leo Baeck writes, each period must win its own Bible.[7] The Bible is the church's book.

The uses of Scripture in Pharisaic Christianity move between the rabbinic poles of *haggada* and *halaka*. *Halaka* is commentary on the laws of Scripture, interpreting and applying these laws to conduct. *Haggada* usually is the interpretation of biblical narratives, and is intended to shape the loyalties and dispositions of listeners. To give a New Testament example,[8] if Jesus' prohibition of divorce in Mark 10 is *halaka,* then his words are legislative and to be strictly obeyed in practice. If it is *haggada,* then Jesus was concerned with creating among his followers a readiness not to divorce, even in cases where the Law permitted it.

The use of Scripture oscillates between these poles. On the one hand, the Bible is more than an ethics manual or law-book. It is the ruling source of knowledge of God, which in turn informs and shapes the proper response to God. It is a resource for character formation and an aid to spiritual discernment.[9] With James Gustafson, Pharisaic Christians affirm the "great variety" in the Bible's moral themes and forms of instruction.[10] This is Scripture's "haggadic" use.

But its principal use is "halakic." In Pharisaic Christianity, the most appropriate question to put to biblical texts is not doctrinal but ethical: How should we live? In this generation, what path should the people of God take? What is the intentional and behavioral shape of the way of God? Orthodoxy is orthopraxy. Pharisaic Christianity is halakic Christianity.

Biblical interpretation becomes a continuous search for a *coherent web of laws* to illuminate and define this path. The assumption here is that man's vision is cloudy, and needs outside illumination. Torah law is believed to be akin to a work of art, appealing to the mind, the affections, the attention—"enlightening the eyes" (Psalm 19:8b). It shows us something about the world. It helps us see.

Torah law is not primarily descriptive, however, but imperative. At bottom, it is an address to the will, and its grand assumptions are the waywardness and the freedom of that will. Thus in Pharisaic Christianity, Torah law is not translatable into statements about what God is doing or what he is like (as in the response model), or about God's intentions and goals for the world (teleological model). The essence of Torah law is God's will for human activity—directing the attention of the faithful away from themselves to the One who can break human oppression, who gives the soul protection and stability, and who leads that continuous re-formation that purifies ordinary life without crushing it (Psalm 119:89–104, 114, 134).

2. Theology: Proceeds "From Below"

The central problem in Christian theology is Christology, or giving an account of Jesus and his relation to God. There are two Christological methods common in modern dogmatics, and the choice here both reflects and affects one's entire theological structure. One method begins "from above," from the divinity of Jesus and the concept of the Incarnation. Assuming that God's Son has descended from heaven to become man in Jesus, this approach asks exactly how God assumed human nature. In the ancient and the modern church, the conceptual structure of most theology "from above" has paralleled the gnostic redeemer myth of the descent of the redeemer from heaven and his return there.

Christology "from below" moves in the opposite direction, rising from the historical man Jesus to the recognition of his divinity. Instead of presupposing Jesus' divinity, this method focuses on the life and message of Jesus of Nazareth, on his manifold relations with the Judaism and Hellenism of his time, and asks what there was in his appearance that led to a recognition of his divinity, i.e., to the doctrine of the Incarnation. Christology "from below" is the natural approach of Pharisaic Christian theology, which emphasizes the humanity of Jesus and his teachings more than his person.[11]

Doing theology "from below" is as congenial to Pharisaic Christianity now as it was for primitive Jewish Christianity, because both display that lively Judaic suspicion of theology undisciplined by biblical revelation. Finite man is like the grass that withers and fades; nothing he has or knows is even comparable to the Creator God of the Bible, to whom the world's inhabitants are "like grasshoppers," and before whom even all the nations together are "less than nothing and emptiness" (Isaiah 40). These two convictions—that God's mysterious absolute will is beyond human discovery, and that his revealed Word is man's portion—combine to produce a striking lack of interest in theological speculation. Neusner notes the absence of philosophical questions and historical visions in Pharisaic writings, which contrasts sharply with the writings of other ancient Palestinian sects.[12]

This special temper pervades the entire position of Pharisaic Christianity, giving it an almost prophetic sensitivity to pretension in alternative world views, even in Christian ones that complement it. For example: to speak of God becoming man, to attempt to follow and elaborate God's Son's way into the world, Wolfhart Pannenberg argues, is usually to claim a rather marked proximity to the position of God himself! What God is apart from the man Jesus "completely escapes our imagination."[13] This same disposition toward in-house iconoclasm appears in the early work of Karl Barth—with its stress on the distance between the creature and the Creator, its critique of *theologia gloriae* (theology of glory) as flight from God's judgment and an ingenious symbol of church domination, its portrait of the relativity and worldliness of "the strange new world within the Bible," and the like.[14] It appears as well in the historical work of Reinhold Niebuhr, particularly where he chooses the category of *irony* to criticize both the liberal and Marxist dreams of bringing the whole of human history under the control of the human will. He writes:

> The whole drama of human history is under the scrutiny of a divine judge who laughs at human pretensions without being hostile to human aspirations. The laughter at the pretensions is divine judgment. The judgment is transmuted into mercy if it results in abating the pretensions and in prompting men to a contrite recognition of the vanity of their imagination.[15]

The temper of Pharisaic Christianity, then, is this-worldly, and its antipathy to gnostic flights toward heaven is quite natural. The Christian gnostic practice of limiting the universal range of redemption in Christ to a spiritual elite was, after all, based in two, fairly clear doctrines; and both of them are anathema in Pharisaic Christian theology. The first was that Redemption is properly conceived as separate from Creation, because human fulfillment lies outside the evil, finite world. The second was an emphasis on the control of the spirit over the body, associating virtue with a higher knowledge or freedom rather than with obedience.[16]

3. Ethics: Deontological View of the Moral Life

To center Christian ethics on law and on divine moral commands is unpopular today, particularly in Protestant circles. Surely, we are told, to require men and women to submit to moral direction "imposed" from without is ethically primitive, suitable perhaps for children but never for mature adults. Yet this is precisely the position of Pharisaic Christianity. The moral life is the obedient life. Ethics is studying, interpreting and applying the Law, i.e., the revealed will of the living God. To this position life without law is *inconceivable,* because it would entail the elimination not only of morality but also of God. Naturalistic attacks on the authority of Law in morality, such as the ethical work of Paul Tillich, meet in Pharisaic Christianity an implacable enemy.[17]

Such "legalism" in morals and sanctification is associated with the conviction that certain actions carry moral qualities in themselves more important than either the consequences flowing from them or the intentions of the actor(s) involved.[18] Though obeying divine Law is believed to be good (as well as right) and to bring a reward, the Pharisaic Christian ethic of obedience does not flirt with consequentialism. As Bultmann has written on ancient Jewish ethics, concerns about consequences are subordinate ethically to the value of the obedient act itself.[19]

The same point can be made about the status of *intentions* in this system. While the Law itself attends to them (e.g., Matthew 5–7), psychoanalytical and confessional data about intentions are not considered to be particularly reliable. In halakic ethics, the self that others can see is ultimately the real self. The "inner man," as a discrete subject for moral assessment, does not exist. With Willard Gaylin, Pharisaic Christians find the revelation that a drug-pusher's heart has been in the right place all along to be interesting, but *not* a substitute for his behavior in describing him.[20]

Underlying this deontology is a "pessimistic" view of the human condition, for Pharisaic Christianity believes human nature to be sinful or fallen. Richard Mouw argues that there are two aspects of this condition with special relevance to an ethic of divine moral commands.[21] The first is the role of self-deception in personal and social life. "The heart is deceitful above all things, and desperately corrupt; who can understand it?" (Jeremiah 17:9). Self-deception extends into all spheres of human activity, including the moral sphere where it takes the form of "rationalization"—the inventing of reasons for doing what ought not to be done and for not doing what ought to be done. The only exit from self-deception—Pharisaic Christians believe—is through understanding oneself in light of an external, transcendent standard: Torah law. This is why two biblical metaphors for the Law are the sun and a lamp for our feet (Psalm 19:4ff; 119:105).

The second relevant aspect of human fallenness, Mouw writes, is vulnerability. A characteristic shape of sin is the perverse use of human strength to exploit human weakness. No one is without vulnerability, and no one is without tendencies to exploit vulnerability.

Men and women need protection from themselves. And the Law, of course, is believed to play a key role in this protection.

It is with some hesitation that I have called the Pharisaic Christian view of the human condition "pessimistic," but over against the view that modern men have outgrown the need for divine commands, or against the view that man is perfectible to a state beyond the Law, it surely is that. To Pharisaic Christians, neither objectivity nor unselfishness is natural to human beings. Man's vision is clouded, and needs outside illumination. Man's will is perverse and rebellious, needing outside correction. Now many Christians undoubtedly will call this pessimism. But some, almost instinctively, will call it realism.

4. Politics: The Tradition of Political Realism

The following six chapters (3-8) suggest a posture Pharisaic Christians might take on particular issues. But predicting the political position of any *group* of Christians is risky, regardless of their stripe, partly because of the force of circumstances in all political judgments. The uncertainty and unpredictable variety of life makes this sort of prediction tenuous at best. Nonetheless, the biblical and theological position of Pharisaic Christianity does provide the foundation for a political philosophy falling within the grand tradition of political realism.

What is political realism? Its formative Christian roots go back to the mind of the North African Augustine, particularly to his penetrating studies of the will and to the doctrines of the "two kingdoms" and of "original sin." In twentieth century political thought, Hans Morgenthau and Reinhold Niebuhr have been two outstanding representatives. Niebuhr is particularly important for this study because with some help from Kierkegaard and Freud, his attack on modern utopianism and Greek individual perfectionism was based squarely on the traditional Judeo-Christian view of man.

At the heart of political realism is a "double refusal," and it appears as clearly in the pages of a fifteenth century pioneer like Machiavelli as in Niebuhr's work. On the one hand, there is a recurrent tendency in social thought to separate religious and political morality—either by dismissing the turmoil of politics as thoroughly evil or unreal and proposing withdrawal into religious conventicles, or by embracing the political process as the most reliable source of practical guidance and dismissing the strictures of religion as naive idealism. The yogi and the commissar go their separate ways. The first mark of political realism is its refusal to accept this separation. Both Christian standards of good and evil and the values sought after in political activity are sanctioned as genuine and important.

But there is an equally firm refusal to harmonize them. The genius of this tradition of political realism lies in the creative tension it maintains between these two quite different strategies for dealing with fallen human beings. Political philosophy is not just a branch of religious or moral philosophy, though many have treated it as such. At best, argues the tradition, religion and politics complement each other, religion providing the strongest personal check on selfishness, and politics its most effective social constraint. The two strategies should thus never be identified or confused. Better to accept a "frank dualism in morals," Niebuhr wrote, "than to attempt a harmony between the two methods that threatens the effectiveness of both."[22]

The political philosophy of Pharisaic Christianity falls within the parameters of this tradition. Its rather strict deontology and "pessimistic" view of the human condition lead to the position that the restraining use of the Law is permanent everywhere. They believe this is particularly true in the public realm, not because politicians are uncommonly evil and certainly not because the pious need Law any less, but because there the Torah's author is not explicitly recognized, and its content not fully honored. They naturally oppose any form of gnosticism which, by identifying perfection with a state beyond the Law, tends to devalue the Law's negative function.

They resist religiously-inspired conservative movements that advocate withdrawal based on perfectionist or other types of otherworldly denigration of public life. The Pharisees of old did not follow the Essenes' example, for they refused to separate Redemption from the whole of Creation and believed too deeply in human freedom and in the coming Kingdom of God. Their descendants do likewise.

On the other hand, the theological empiricism (theology from below) among Pharisaic Christians makes them just as suspicious of the left-wing version of this dualism, namely the apocalyptic denigration of the existing order on behalf of a New Kingdom. Politically, they find descendants of the Zealots hardly to be preferred to those of the Essenes. At two points, however, there is some political agreement between Pharisaic and Apocalyptic Christianity—about the pervasiveness of evil, and about the weakness of unaided human agency in bringing about God's Kingdom.

Predictably, the vision of the Kingdom in Pharisaic Christianity is in terms of the universal "rule of God's Law." More than any other single factor, this deontological vision of the Kingdom is responsible for making them lean politically toward various forms of constitutionalism, where personal freedom is protected by a written compendium of laws that "rule the rulers." We have noted that in their community structure, the Bible is treated as a constitution *intra muros.* So despite their emphasis on order and law, there is no opening in Pharisaic Christianity—as there manifestly is in some modern conservatism—for flirtation with totalitarianism or fascism.[23]

If there is a note of conservatism in this political philosophy, and indeed there is, it does not spring from a principled interest in preserving some status quo. After all, the Pharisees drew much of their inspiration from the Hebrew prophets. Rather, it is akin to the conservatism to which the liberal Niebuhr confessed in 1956,[24] and it emerges clearly in the Pharisaic Christian view of social change.

Since Edmund Burke, Anglo-Saxon conservative thought has been marked by its appreciation of the organic, unintended factors in social life, and has consistently opposed "social contract" theories which—by applying voluntaristic symbols of making and designing to social origins—neglect and obscure precisely these factors. To be sure, one function of such theories in the thought of Hobbes, Rousseau and others has always been to recall men to a responsible exercise of their social freedom, and with this Pharisaic Christians have no quarrel. But the basic claim of social contract theory is that present societies are the *intended product of human will;* men can "remake" them now because they "created" them originally. "Ultimately considered," Niebuhr argued, "this is a religious issue. For the extreme voluntarism is related to a lack of appreciation of the providential factors in community building."[25]

This is the sort of conservatism one is likely to find among Pharisaic Christians. Their stress on human limitations together with the belief that all history and human agency is "ruled by" divine providence inoculates them against excessively voluntaristic accounts of social change or stability. Such accounts appear at once impious and olympian. Society is *affected* by the human will, they believe, and it is the business of social ethics to investigate the manner and means of this effect; but in no evident sense is society simply its product.

5. Ecclesiology: Sharp Distinction Between the Church and the World

"Let the church be the church!"was a rallying cry in ecumenical circles not long ago, and it remains a useful summary of the Pharisaic Christian conception of Christian mission. Let the church *be* the church. What the church is to do in and for the world is first of all to continually recover what God is calling it to be. And the *sine qua non* of God's call to his church is to be holy (Leviticus 19) or, in some sense or other, *separate*. This conception of the church, therefore, entails a sharp distinction between the church and the world.

The basis of the distinction is located, once again, in the Law. The church's key problem today is perceived as the ancient one of being far too worldly to influence the world. "You shall not do," God said to Moses in the desert,

> as they do in the land of Egypt, where you dwelt, [or in] . . . Canaan, to which I am bringing you. You shall not walk in their statutes. You shall do my ordinances and keep my statutes and walk in them. I am the Lord your God. You shall therefore keep my statutes and my ordinances, by doing which a man shall live: I am the Lord (Leviticus 18:3–5).

Thus, it is through his Law that God both enjoins and structures the church's liberation from cultural captivity. From the standpoint of God's people, there does not appear to be anything optional about this use of the Law that Calvinists have dubbed its third or "didactic" use. Without it, the salt will quickly lose its savor (Matthew 5); without it in a storm, the house of faith itself may begin to crumble, not—as it appears—because of the storm's power, but because of an earlier and foolish decision to build the house on sand instead of rock (Matthew 7).

In Pharisaic Christianity, the Torah is believed to be the leading instrument of one of God's deepest purposes in the world, which is to call out a peculiar people to anticipate his coming Kingdom. The church's vision of itself is to be shaped by the doctrine of election; it is a "chosen race, a royal priesthood, a holy nation, a people for God's possession" (1 Peter 2:9). For Christians, in short, the prerequisite of effective love and service in the the world is that they must first "leave" it. So the political realism among Pharisaic Christians is combined with a type of ecclesiological perfectionism. It is thus most unlikely that they will tolerate that fatal perversion of realism, in which the insight into human selfishness and evil is so stressed as to cut the ethical nerve, making what is merely universal in human behavior normative as well.

The view of perfection in Pharisaic Christianity is controlled by its view of the Kingdom of God. Pharisaic Christians are legal perfectionists, conceiving of the Kingdom in terms of obedience to law. It is the Torah law to which—they believe—every human being that breathes is subject. Explicit here is the categorical denial of a "double church morality,"[26] i.e., one morality for the world and another for the congregation, one for the heathen and another for Christians. The difference between the church and the world does not lie in the standard applied to them; it is the same Torah law. It lies in their differing responses to the standard's Author. For those outside the worshiping community, the Torah is at best a challenge but usually a threat, the ominous voice of a distant enemy. Inside, the Torah—written and oral—is part of God's gracious leading of his people; its commandments no longer threaten life at its edges but gently shape it from its center, giving it a clear direction, an inner continuity and a firm security even in the face of death.[27]

So the essential task of the church in the world is to become what it is: an anticipation of the Kingdom, leaven, salt. Pharisaic Christians are usually far too realistic about *themselves* to believe that this anticipation will ever be anything more than fragmentary.[28] But they live in hope that it may become more perfect than it is. The internal structure or order of the church is thus always a *de fide* question, and it is so exactly in the context of mission. As Richard Mouw has written, the mission of the church is to be found neither solely inside itself nor exclusively in action out in the world. Rather it is to be God's "showpiece" wherein the church shares with the world the transformed life to which God, through the church, calls men.[29]

NOTES

1. See George Strecker's essay "On the Problem of Jewish Christianity" in Walter Bauer, *Orthodoxy and Heresy in Earliest Christianity.* Kraft and Krodel, eds. (Philadelphia, 1971), pp. 241–285.

2. Brevard Childs, *Biblical Theology in Crisis* (Philadelphia, 1970), p. 136.

3. Harold Lindsell, *The Battle for the Bible* (Grand Rapids, 1976).

4. Jack T. Sanders, *Ethics in the New Testament* (Philadelphia, 1975).

5. Norman Lamm, *Faith and Doubt: Studies in Traditional Jewish Thought* (New York, 1971).

6. See Calvin's exposition of the moral law's three uses in *Institutes of the Christian Religion,* John T. McNeill, ed. (Philadelphia, 1960), Bk. II, ch. vii, pars. 6–13.

7. Leo Baeck, *The Essence of Judaism* (London, 1936), p. 17.

8. Suggested by Allen Verhey in his article, "Divorce," *International Standard Bible Encyclopedia,* Vol. I (Grand Rapids, 1979), p. 976.

9. The importance of character formation in the biblical contribution to Christian ethics is a prominent theme in Bruce C. Birch and Larry Rasmussen, *Bible and Ethics in the Christian Life* (Minneapolis, 1976).

10. James Gustafson, "The Place of Scripture in Christian Ethics: A Methodological Study," *Interpretation,* 24/4, pp. 430–55.

11. Cf. the contrast between the Jewish and Hellensitic contributions to early Christianity nicely summarized in G. H. C. MacGregor and A. C. Purdy, *Jew and Greek: Tutors Unto Christ* (London, 1936).

12. Jacob Neusner, *Rabbinic Traditions,* III, pp. 77–78.

13. Wolfhart Pannenberg, *Jesus—God and Man,* Wilkins and Priebe, trs. (London, 1968), p. 38.

14. All these themes are in Karl Barth, *The Word of God and The Word of Man*, Horton, tr. (London, 1928).

15. Reinhold Niebuhr, *The Irony of American History* (New York, 1952), p. 155.

16. Iris Murdoch finds this second emphasis in the existentialist-beha-

viorist view of the self that lies behind much contemporary moral philosophy. See her attack on this view in *The Sovereignty of the Good* (London, 1970).

17. Calling the law "arbitrary" and "strange" does not disguise the fact that Tillich wants to do away with divine external standards as such, and not just inappropriate ones: Paul Tillich, *Morality and Beyond* (New York, 1963), p. 24. On the value of law as part of "structures that embody the experience and wisdom of the past" (p. 93), he appears to take a different position.

18. This is the position of Lewis B. Smedes in his fine book *Sex for Christians* (Grand Rapids, 1976).

19. Rudolf Bultmann, *Jesus and the Word,* Smith and Huntress, trs. (New York, 1934), Ch. 3.

20. Willard Gaylin, "What You See Is the Real You," *Hastings Center Report* (October 1977).

21. Richard J. Mouw, "Commands for Grown-Ups," *Worldview* (July 1972), pp. 38ff.

22. Reinhold Niebuhr, *Moral Man and Immoral Society* (New York, 1932), p. 271. On his indebtedness to Augustine, see his "Augustine's Political Realism," *Christian Realism and Political Problems* (London, 1954), pp. 114–39.

23. See Noël O'Sullivan's careful critique of T. S. Eliot and Christopher Dawson in *Conservatism* (London, 1976), pp. 134–38.

24. Reinhold Niebuhr, "Reply to Interpretation and Criticism," *Reinhold Niebuhr: His Religious, Social and Political Thought,* Charles W. Kegley and Robert W. Bretall, eds. (New York 1956), p. 434.

25. *Ibid.* F. A. Hayek's blistering attack on the social contract theory in *The Constitution of Liberty* (Chicago, 1960) is a goldmine of legal and political information, but omits the religious issue. On this point, see John Yoder's comments on Christian attempts to help God manage history in *The Politics of Jesus* (Grand Rapids, 1972), Ch. 12.

26. Cf. Dietrich Bonhoeffer, *Ethics,* p. 358.

27. There is in this tradition therefore no *necessary* contradiction between (even legal) constraint and the experience of grace. J. Gustafson's carefully worded criticism of Christian legal ethics within the theme of "Jesus Christ, the Pattern" suffers from his persistent refusal to consider that some Christians may see in Christ both an external moral authority *and* God's revelation of his love and forgiveness: *Christ and the Moral Life* (New York, 1968), pp. 183–87. I suspect that Gustafson's analytical agenda—to concentrate on discrete ethical themes rather than the full theology of writers—may amplify this refusal in the section noted, for earlier in the book (p.

115) he uses exactly this point to criticize Christian ethicists who oversimplify the efficacy of grace.

28. In the Strasbourg version of the worship liturgy in early Calvinism, the singing of each commandment in the Decalogue ended with the refrain "Kyrie, Eleison" (Lord, have mercy). Thus even where the reading of divine law is clearly an act of praise and gratitude (not a call to confession), there is an equally clear recognition that what the law defines is an obedience that no one is acting out perfectly or completely: Howard Hageman, "The Law in the Liturgy," p. 43.

29. Richard J. Mouw, *Political Evangelism* (Grand Rapids, 1973), p. 41. In a later book, he elaborates some of the complexity of this "showpiece" concept: *Politics and the Biblical Drama* (Grand Rapids, 1976), Ch. 4.

III

THE LAW OF WORSHIP

Remember the sabbath day, and keep it holy.
                                        Exodus 20:8

And one of the scribes . . . seeing that he answered them well,
asked him, "Which commandment is the first of all?" Jesus
answered, "The first is, 'Hear, O Israel: The Lord our God,
the Lord is one; and you shall love the Lord your God with all
your heart, and with all your soul, and with all your mind,
and with all your strength.' The second is this, 'You shall love
your neighbor as yourself.' There is no other commandment
greater than these." And the scribe said to him, "You are
right, Teacher; you have truly said that he is one, and there is
no other but he; and to love him with all the heart, and with
all the understanding, and with all the strength, and to love
one's neighbor as oneself, is much more than all whole burnt
offerings and sacrifices." And when Jesus saw that he answered wisely, he said to him, "You are not far from the kingdom of God." And after that no one dared to ask him any
question.

                                        Mark 12:28–34

For Pharisaic Christianity, the Great Commandment is the ethical center of the New Testament and, by extension, of Christianity as
a whole.[1] Mark's account of Jesus' formulation is particularly important, since unlike the parallels in Matthew (22:32–40) and Luke
(10:25–37), the relationship between Jesus and his Jewish questioner
(probably a Pharisee)[2] is portrayed here as a sympathetic one. On the

one hand, it is no wonder that Jesus commends the scribe for his response, for in it he not only affirms what Jesus says but expands it by showing the Commandment's force as an attack on idolatry ("there is no other but he") and false piety ("much more than . . . burnt offerings and sacrifices"). On the other hand, we might expect the Jewish community to be receptive since Jesus is simply quoting two well-known Torah texts—Deuteronomy 6:4 (The Shema) and Leviticus 19:18.

But the combination of the two texts in Jesus' teaching was a distinctive feature. Though Hillel is recorded to have summed up the Law as not doing to others what you would not have them do to you, I have seen no evidence for a combination of the two texts before the time of Jesus. Pharisaic Christians regard Jesus' statement as the *supreme* commandment in that it summarizes and comprehends all other divine commandments. This supremacy over the other commandments, then, is not understood to mean relaxing, changing, or superseding them.[3] In the words of the letter of James, it is the "royal law" exactly in the sense that it is the "whole law" (James 2:8–10).

It is also the most radical of commandments, because it reveals the root of all ethical guidance worthy of the name "Christian." On it depend not only the Law in its entirety but the prophets as well (Matthew 22:40). Through it, morality is given an irreducibly religious, monotheistic foundation. The Great Commandment cuts like a mighty, two-edged sword through the life of the Christian community—uprooting, purifying and guiding Christians in the most distinctive, native activities for which God's grace frees them: worship, prayer, love of neighbor.[4]

Much of the Great Commandment's power lies in what might be called its "binitarian" form. Though the Commandment has two parts, Jesus presents them together as the rule that is "first of all." Here is the Law's heart and soul, and to separate its components is inevitably to disable it. Neither should the parts be ranked, one above the other. The text iself overrules this: Jesus does not rank the two commands, but lists them, giving each component equal and related importance.[5] The Great Commandment is a *single* commandment. As the Lord is one, so is his Law, which would be the

Pharisaic Christian reading of Augustine's famous dictum, "Love God, and do as you please."

On the other hand, the two parts of the Commandment are each distinct commands, claiming man in different ways and pointing him in different directions. What Jesus told the scribe, in fact, is that *no* single command constitutes the essence of the Law and stands above all the other requirements; only a dual commandment will serve that purpose. The formulation of Jesus is thus not only two in one, but one in *two,* and herein lies the Great Commandment's prophetic potency. For this Commandment beyond the commandments cuts two ways. It exposes the false piety of Christian "verticalists" who subordinate love of neighbor to what they call "religion." And it uncovers the idolatry of Christian "horizontalists" who are so impressed with modern political power and with secular critiques of religion that they deny the religious foundation of morality, and end up embracing the rationalist heresy that worship is not really necessary.

In contrast to modern, secular assumptions, biblical thought proposes that man is *homo adorans.* The urge to both adore heroes or gods and identify with them is understood to be rooted so deeply in human nature that worship is not only necessary but innate, as natural to the human species as eating and sexual communion. Ernest Becker is quite right that in any particular society, the expression of this ubiquitous aptitude is governed largely by "the way society sets up its hero system and in the people it allows to fill its roles."[6] But final responsibility for the attitude does not lie with society. The culprit is God who creates people that way (i.e., to worship him) but with the freedom to choose other objects or powers such as race, a nation, a family, a system of rewards (the "bitch goddess"), or perhaps simply oneself. Whether people become religious or not depends on which object they choose, but the inclination to worship as such is considered fundamental. As the Great Commandment suggests, a person's worship is so basic that it affects all realms of life, including morality. This is why idolatry is a central category in the Old Testament, and never exclusively a religious one.

The human propensity to worship has *political* consequences as well, and the resulting behavior has not escaped the attention of social analysts. In a gloomy, perceptive book, Robert Heilbroner criticizes leftist views of power that skirt careful examination of that upon which all effective political power is based: consent. Heilbroner focuses on the impulse to identify with one's nation and on political obedience—that "perplexing readiness, even eagerness, with which authority is accepted by the vast majority" in any society; that persistent "hunger for 'leadership'" from someplace higher. He locates the source of both traits in infantile and early family experiences, which for him explains the inordinate power of political "parental" figures who can re-create the emotional and psychological custody of one's early years.[7]

History provides abundant evidence of man's *need* to worship, and we might be tempted to conclude that worship becomes true as and to the degree that it meets man's need. At least with respect to Christian worship, this conclusion is false. No utilitarian or functional framework can adequately clarify the meaning of worship, because its essential purpose is not determined by man at all, but by the nature and will of its object: God the Father, Son, and Holy Spirit.

How, then, does Christian theology understand Christian worship? In the first place, divine worship is an end in itself.[8] With the evangelization of the world, it is one of the two great ends of the Christian church. It would be quite mistaken to conceive of worship as instrumental to *anything*—to human rights, to peace of mind or soul, to liberation, even to love of neighbor. The Great Commandment, remember, has two parts which are not to be ranked or fused. On this point, confusion is often greatest inside the church. Sunday morning worship is typically and wrongly construed as a spiritual "filling station," where Christians are cleansed and endowed with blessings and grace to live their lives through the working week. These may well be among its *effects.* But worship in spirit and in truth seeks nothing more than the beauty and glory of the Father. Christians worship because it is commanded, yes, but even more: simply because they find themselves free to do so. The glorification of God is "the most characteristic act of man."[9]

In the second place, genuine worship is always eucharistic, the act in which the faithful community "is caught up in freedom, love, joy, and self-surrender, into the once-for-all and eternal sacrifice of Christ."[10] The Son reveals that the nature of God is love (1 John 4:8):

"for God so loved the world that he gave his only Son" (John 3:16a).
The Son also reveals what this "love" is; for Christ Jesus

> emptied himself, taking the form of a servant, being born in
> the likeness of men. And being found in human form he
> humbled himself and became obedient unto death, even
> death on a cross. Therefore God has highly exalted him
> and bestowed on him the name which is above every name,
> that at the name of Jesus every knee shall bow, in heaven
> and on earth and under the earth, and every tongue confess
> that Jesus Christ is Lord, to the glory of God the Father.
> (Philippians 2:7–11)

In relation to this unparalleled act of Jesus—the perfect sacrifice—
sacrifices in other religions appear as types and shadows. This is why
the Christian tradition so identifies worship with the celebration of
the Eucharist or Lord's Supper. To worship is precisely to share in
the sacrifice of God's Son. It is to be fed by the Body and Blood of
Christ. It is to respond to God's mercy by presenting oneself as a living sacrifice, holy and acceptable unto God (Romans 12:1).

While it is true that the Great Commandment illuminates and
gives form to this response, it is perhaps more true that the sacrifice
of God's Son is the context in which the Great Commandment itself
should be understood. Jesus tells the scribe that we are to love God
and neighbor, but the text as such reveals neither the source of this
love nor its controlling definition. To Jews and Christians, God's
loving-kindness and mercy are the source of love, so much so that
John's claim in his first letter is not an exaggeration: "He who loves
is born of God and knows God" (1 John 4:7). Love is a miracle. The
tragedy of love is that it remains a *rare* miracle in a fallen world,
where the preoccupation with self among men and women invests finite claims with tyrannical power (idolatry), thereby alienating them
from the divine command which contains at once the truth about
themselves and the only way to freedom. Victor Furnish rightly describes the Great Commandment as a "command inherent in a
gift."[11]

And what is love? John's first letter continues with the argument that the controlling criterion of love is the sacrifice of God's Son. It is not love that is God; God is love. "In this is love, not that we loved God but that he loved us and sent his Son to be the expiation of our sins" (1 John 4:10). God's love is not only a prior gift enabling the love that he claims, liberating men and women from bondage to self and to the world; divine love alone is the eternal measure of what this love is. It therefore quite properly should shape the response to the Great Commandment.

But to locate the Commandment in the context of worship and the sacrifice of God's Son doesn't change its status as a *commandment.* The summons to love God and neighbor does not arise from within the natural affections of the commanded one, or from the attractiveness of the one to be loved. Sacrificial love, as distinct from and often opposed to *eros,* is summoned by a source outside the parties to the relationship. Love in the Christian sense remains commanded by God, which means it is usually not something "spontaneous" but rather must continually be called forth.[12]

In the third place, and perhaps most mysteriously, divine worship is an act of the Holy Spirit operating through man as a free being.[13] This is most visible today in the charismatic movement, but charismatics have simply in their own way recovered an element essential to all Christian worship. The very origin of the Christian church, the Body of Christ, is the descent of the Holy Spirit at Pentecost. Apart from the Spirit there would be no church, no worship, no prayer. Writes Paul: "We do not know how to pray as we ought, but the Spirit himself intercedes for us with sighs too deep for words" (Romans 8:26). "Do you not know that you are God's temple and that God's Spirit dwells in you? . . . God's temple is holy, and that temple you are" (1 Corinthians 3:16, 18). Unlike the spirits of the world, the Holy Spirit is always the spirit of freedom (2 Corinthians 3:17). Thus James is not playing with words when he calls divine law "the law of liberty" (James 2:12). In Pharisaic Christianity, likewise, it only appears to be the case that Christian freedom is somehow equated with obedience, though this is close to the truth. Freedom for Pharisaic Christians is to be called to obedience by *God.*

We are now in a better position to consider the quite practical question of the significance of Sunday. The attitude of Jesus toward the sabbath is of particular importance here. The gospels suggest that Jesus clearly preferred it as a day for messianic work. i.e., for performing miracles and preaching in the synagogues. It was the day, he explained to the Jews, when "my Father is working still, and I am working" (John 5:17). When Jesus proclaimed himself "lord of the Sabbath" (Matthew 12:8), he is often interpreted as expressing ethical opposition to—here we are again—nasty Jewish legalism and formalism. But such a construction misses the mark. Jesus' attitude toward the sabbath was overtly eschatological. The Jewish sabbath looked toward and anticipated the age to come, the proclamation of God's immanent rule, the perfecting of the covenant, and the coming of the Messiah—all of which Jesus saw in himself.[14] He was indeed the sabbath's "Lord." In Matthew 12, it is this messianic issue that divided Jesus and the Pharisees; since they knew sabbath history and law so well, Jesus argued, they of all people should recognize who he was. But some didn't. "I tell you, something greater than the temple is here" (v. 6).

In Jesus, early Christians found the true temple and true sabbath rest, and therefore their day of worship could not remain the sabbath day. It had to be a different day, the "first day of the week" (Acts 20:7), or the day after the old sabbath, the day when Jesus rose again from the dead (Matthew 28:1). For Christians to have maintained the sabbath of the Jews would have been the most explicit possible testimony that the Messiah had not actually come.

As time passed, the Christian church discovered Sunday to be a day of worship *par excellence,* looking backward and looking forward, as commemoration and as anticipation. Each Sunday is an Easter day. On that day the church in worship recalls and celebrates those events which brought it into existence, Christ's victory over death and the outpouring of the Holy Spirit. It must be Sunday because only this day evokes the great new beginning, the triumphal appearance of a future other than death. In its weekly celebration the church both announces and experiences ever anew the significance of Easter.[15]

But Sunday is special as well because it embodies the future. In Sunday worship the church anticipates and looks forward to the final "day of the Lord" that has become the "day of Jesus Christ" (Philippians 1:6)—when the Father's name will be hallowed, when his

Kingdom will come, when at the name of his Son Jesus every knee
will bow and every tongue confess his Lordship. This day, however,
is *not yet*. So the French liturgiologist von Allmen wants the eschatological tension between Sunday and non-eucharistic days to be strictly maintained.[16] Otherwise the church's situation in time is
profoundly falsified, by obscuring (or in effect denying) either the
fallen world or the presence of God's Kingdom. Sunday worship
clearly testifies to the presence here and now of the age to come; to
negate this is to empty Easter and Pentecost of their reality. But the
new age is received only by people of faith. Every day is not yet a
Sunday.

It should now be clear that what sanctifies Sunday is worship,
not rest. From the time of Constantine, when the Emperor declared
that the day of the sun should be a holiday, Sunday began to attract
to itself the idea of a Christian "sabbath," a social day of rest. In fact,
however, there is a deep and abiding tension between the Christian
day of worship and a weekly day of rest. The contradictions emerged
most dramatically in seventeenth and eighteenth century Protestantism, particularly in Britain and the Netherlands, where Sunday observance lapsed into a strict sabbatarian legalism, a pattern clearly at
variance with the early Christian view of Sunday as a day of triumph
and liberty. Cessation from work is not what sanctifies Sunday; and
thus the world, with its protective laws, can't help. It is rather Sunday which, in its worship, sanctifies the world's day and all other
days.[17]

Finally, Sunday worship can be seen as a rite honoring the highest of sacrifices, the sacrifice of love. In Pharisaic Christianity, this
means it must also be the cult of the divine command. For then it
will be a festival of freedom. "Only when it is a duty to love," wrote
Kierkegaard, "only then is love . . . emancipated in blessed independence."

> If one man, when another says to him, "I can no longer
> love you," proudly answers, "Then I can also stop loving
> you": is this independence? Alas, it is only dependence, for
> the fact as to whether he will continue to love or not de-
> pends on whether the other will love. But the one who an-

swers, "Then I *will* still continue to love you," his love is everlastingly free in blessed independence. He does not say it proudly—dependent on his pride; no, he says it humbly, humbling himself under the "shalt" of eternity, and just for that reason he is independent.[18]

NOTES

1. This does not entail the claim that it is the center of the New Testament itself, which is much more interested in Christ crucified than in ethics as such.

2. R. McL. Wilson, "Mark," *Peake's Commentary on the Bible,* Matthew Black, ed. (New York, 1962), p. 812.

3. Cf. the intended effect of Joseph Fletcher's position that the Great Commandment is a "distillation" of the "spirit and ethos of many laws" which "liberates" their intention: *Situation Ethics: The New Morality* (Philadelphia, 1966), pp. 70–71.

4. The ablest modern defense of the thesis that Christian worship has equal *ethical* status with service and love of neighbor is still probably Kenneth E. Kirk's classic, *The Vision of God* (London, 1931). In the abridged edition (Cambridge, 1977), see particularly "Jewish Anticipations" (pp. 9–16) and "Law and Promise" (pp. 170–201).

5. See Victor P. Furnish, *The Love Command in the New Testament* (New York, 1972), p. 27.

6. Ernest Becker, *The Denial of Death* (New York, 1973), p. 4.

7. Robert Heilbroner, *An Inquiry into the Human Prospect* (New York, 1974), pp. 106–09.

8. The following framework for understanding worship is drawn from Paul Verghese, *The Joy of Freedom: Eastern Worship and Modern Man* (London, 1967), pp. 20–24.

9. *Ibid.,* p. 21.

10. *Ibid.,* p. 22.

11. Furnish, *op cit.,* p. 207.

12. It is a peculiar virtue of Rudolf Bultmann's ethical work, as in *Jesus and the Word,* that it stresses this "Judaic" quality of biblical Christian ethics.

13. Verghese, *op cit.,* p. 22.

14. Jesus' attitude toward the sabbath appears to me to constitute outstanding evidence that he knew himself to be the Messiah.

15. J. J. von Allmen, *Worship: Its Theology and Practice,* Knight and Fleet, trs. (London, 1965), pp. 219–21.

16. *Ibid.,* p. 223.

17. *Ibid.,* p. 225.

18. Soren Kierkegaard, *The Works of Love,* Swenson tr. (Princeton, 1946), pp. 25, 33.

IV

THE LAW OF GOVERNMENT[1]

> Let every person be subject to the governing authorities. For
> there is no authority except from God, and those that exist
> have been instituted by God. Therefore he who resists the au-
> thorities resists what God has appointed, and those who resist
> will incur judgment. For rulers are not a terror to good con-
> duct but to bad. Would you have no fear of him who is in au-
> thority? Then do what is good, and you will receive his
> approval, for he is God's servant for your good.
>
> Romans 13:1–4

The purpose of the biblical law of government is twofold. Its
critical function is to challenge certain popular and dangerous conceptions of the state as a self-contained entity, existing more or less
independently of biblical revelation. Its constructive function is to
generate Christian theories of the state which are at once grounded
in Scripture and attentive to the wide range of political theory on the
subject. Its summary legal (limiting) content is quoted at the head of
this chapter—those provocative verses from the 13th chapter of
Paul's letter to the church at Rome.

As Bonhoeffer has noted, there are two reigning and important
views of the state in modern political science: a "positive" theory, lo-
cating the state's origins in human nature; and a "negative" theory,
basing it not in man's created nature but in the Fall or sin.[2] The first
is rooted in the ancient Greek concept of the state, particularly in
Aristotle's thought, and attributes great dignity to the political vocation. The state is seen as the highest consummation of the rational
character of man, and to serve it is the supreme purpose of human

life. The negative view, stemming from Augustine and Reformation thought, is a self-conscious attack on the perfectibilism inherent in the Greek concept. It is man's sin, the Reformers argued, not his greatness that leads to the institution of government, which is not established by man at all but by God.

Both of these views, however—that the state is an institution of creation or an institution of preservation—suggest that government now exists by itself with no continuing relation to the revelation of God—and particularly to this revelation as contained in the New Testament. So we are led at once to a careful reading of Romans 13 in the context of the interpretation of this passage in the Christian community over the centuries. The tradition teaches that Romans 13 has an essential framework, what might be called the "beyond politics" position of the Christian movement.

The position has two parts. First, authentic Christianity has always understood itself to be called beyond politics; there is an eschatological, apolitical thrust in the Christian community which was most evident in the anti-institutional, pacifist posture of the early church. Second, Christians do have a role to play in political life, and that is neither to withdraw from politics nor to transform it into something completely new. The first point is made indirectly throughout the New Testament. The second was not elaborated fully until Augustine set forth his "two kingdoms" thesis in the *City of God;* in Scripture it is the peculiar burden of Paul's argument in the first part of Romans 13.

The political implications of Christianity have certainly not been ignored in contemporary scholarship. Charles N. Cochrane's *Christianity and Classical Culture* (1940), Oscar Cullmann's *The State in the New Testament* (1956), John C. Murray's *We Hold These Truths* (1960), S. G. F. Brandon's *Jesus and the Zealots* (1967), John Passmore's *The Perfectibility of Man* (1970), John H. Yoder's *The Politics of Jesus* (1972) and Richard Mouw's *Politics and the Biblical Drama* (1976) are among the more significant recent publications on the subject. But some definition must be given to the word "political."

Politics is a special kind of activity which has existed since the time of the first human communities. Its essence is always plurality, conflict, difference of opinion. To be sure, some sort of agreement is the goal of many political processes. But the reconciliation is by definition temporary. For the political realm is peopled by individuals with hopes, fears and ambitions often at odds with the plans of other individuals. British journalist Henrie Fairlie has written that political decisions involve "interests which conflict, and are hard to reconcile; wills which cannot be commandeered but at best only persuaded; resources which are limited but on which the claims are many; support which must be weighed and reweighed, and may at any time slip away."

When we define politics this way, is there a distinctively Christian assessment of political life? When this question is put to the New Testament, we find the answer moving in two different directions. On the one hand, all of Scripture is firm in its resistance to polytheism, which in this case would mean marking off the public realm as a particularly demonic (or salvific) sphere. One of the most frequent claims in the Bible is that "the Lord your God is one," sovereign in and over all spheres of life, including politics, and demanding obedience there as well as elsewhere.

At the same time there are strong anti-political themes in the New Testament, most clearly in the Johannine and apocalyptic literature. The situation could hardly be otherwise, since the complicity of the Roman and Jewish political establishments in the crucifixion of Jesus was a decisive experience in the memory of early Christians. "The light shines in the darkness. . . . He was in the world, and the world was made through him, yet the world knew him not" (John 1:5, 10). There are even suggestions that the state is demonic (Revelation 13), that politics is "of the world" and to be hated (1 John), and that politicians will never understand Christianity because it is otherworldly (John 18:33–38).

Some Christians have remained sensitive to these themes. The "separationist" doctrine of American Southern Baptists, for instance, is a dramatic elaboration of the antithesis between Christianity and politics, insisting that the best political order is one in which a "wall" exists between church and state. But those who have most fully grasped the *ethical* significance of the New Testament case against politics are Christian pacifists. Their argument is simple and profound. In the synoptic Gospels and especially in the Sermon on the Mount, the way of Jesus is revealed to be the way of peace. "But

I say unto you, Do not resist one who is evil. But if anyone strikes you on the right cheek, turn to him the other also" (Matthew 5:39). The fate of Jesus reveals the true nature of political powers and principalities: they are demonic, violent and out of control; they are unmasked and disarmed only in the mysterious triumph of Christ's crucifixion and resurrection (Colossians 2:8–15). As Tolstoi insisted, Christians are to be deceived neither by Paul's fuzzy thinking in Romans nor by bourgeois apologists for "progressive" government. Christians and the state are *never* allies; following Christ means nonviolent resistance to existing political power. It is "sectarian" groups such as the Quakers and the Mennonites that have seen most clearly the contradiction between Christian morality and the values of a secular society, particularly on the issues of war, national defense, and the promotion of peace.

Once the permanent validity of this suspicion of public power and political institutions is recognized, the significance of Romans 13 becomes clearer. For the antipolitical thrust in the New Testament creates two familiar temptations in the Christian movement: "sleep" and "drunkenness" (1 Thessalonians 5). Marxists are quite correct to use their leader's phrase in naming *these aberrations* an "opiate of the people."[3] "Sleep" is spiritualizing concrete evil, pretending that political injustice and tyranny are of little consequence next to one's own purity of soul and peace of mind. "Drunkenness" is some form of the belief that Christ has already returned, and therefore the end of the world (particularly the overcoming of evil) is at hand. The temptation is either to withdraw from politics altogether, or—on fire with eschatological hope—to attempt to transform politics into a completely new order. Romans 13:1–7 is an attack on eschatological shortcuts.

Part of a section devoted to ethics (Romans 12–15) in Paul's weightiest and most influential letter, the passage contains more than specific advice about the not-altogether-friendly political institutions of Rome. It is nascent political theory concerning the nature and office of government and of civic obligation. Paul's three points, quite carefully phrased, all have to do with *presumption.*

1. The authority of government, from a human point of view, is ideal and permanent. It comes from God, not from human judg-

ments about governments or about this or that public act. This authority may be removed only by God, and he has not yet done so (vv. 1–2). This view of authority checks the anarchistic bent of early Christianity, which Tolstoi correctly saw reflected in the New Testament. Followers of Christ must never revolt against government on principle.

2. The office of government is to order society morally, to punish evil and reward good (vv. 3–7). Notice that when assigning the office of punishment to government, Paul makes no distinction between Christians and non-Christians. Growing persecutions of Christians made this a delicate issue, but his implication is clear: Christians are to presume that the official exercise of government's retributive arm is legitimate, even when used against Christians.

3. As Calvin was one of the first to note, however, civil disobedience can be justified in particular circumstances in which government is violating its office. Paul does not elaborate *how* such a violation might be determined. He simply states what the office of government is, and that Christians must presume existing governments to be legitimate—a position which leaves the burden of proof on resisters.

According to Romans 13, then, the sacred element in public life can be identified with some precision. It is neither power *per se,* nor kings, nor the state, but only and exclusively the *authority to rule.* In d'Entrèves' formula, the doctrine of Romans 13:1–7 is one of "the sacred character of authority, certainly not one of the divinity of power."[4] The deification of political power in general and of monarchs in particular is a pagan doctrine, institutionalized in Hellenistic monarchies and later in the Roman Empire. Christianity has consistently fought both this ancient idea and its modern version—encouraged by Hegel—that the state is divine. The heroic resistance of the Confessing Church movement and of certain Catholic and Free churches to Hitler's Third Reich is but one recent example of this fight.[5]

The exegesis offered here combines two quite different views of Romans 13 that have had wide currency in Christian social thought, though it stresses one more than the other. The first is an "absolutist" reading characteristic of early Christianity. In this interpretation, the emphasis is almost exclusively on the providential character of power. Good or bad, tyrannical or just, all power is of God, and therefore even evil power must be endured. Christian political ethics in such an ethos commends passive obedience or subordination in some form. The position is rooted in a deeply pessimistic attitude toward political life and political institutions, and has contributed mightily to what we have called the negative theory of the state.

This "absolutist" view of power is alive and well in contemporary Christian ethics, and often does not lead where one would expect, i.e., to quietism or withdrawal from politics. It leads rather to a consistent refusal to accept the validity of classical political distinctions in Christian ethics. Jacques Ellul, for example, concludes that every state is founded on and maintained by violence, and that the ancient distinction between violence and force is an invention of lawyers and "totally unjustified."[6] John Yoder suggests that Christians put aside the idea of rebelling only against bad governments. "They should rather rebel against all and subordinate to all. . . . It is the way we share in God's patience with a system we basically reject."[7]

A second reading of Romans 13, the one stressed here, originates with representative political theorists in the Middle Ages.[8] Its point of departure is verse 4, where Paul instructs Christians that any ruler is "God's servant for your good." Only that power which is directed toward what is good, argues this theory, comes from God. The key assumption is that since the *use* to which political power is put reflects its true character, a distinction can and must always be made between what God ordains and merely human governance. Action reflects being. When a ruler's use of power is founded on justice, it has sacred authority, and the ruler is—even when he doesn't know it—God's minister. What this interpretation does is give legitimacy to a certain form of power, force exercised according to law; it thus might be called a "legalist" view of power.

Such a view dovetails naturally with Aristotle's conception of the relation between law and the state, over against the position of Plato who preferred "government by men" to "government by laws." Though he conceded late in life that there was practical value in the rule of law, Plato's ideal remained teleological, i.e., of a government founded not upon law but upon a rational knowledge of the good. It is finally the pursuit of the good that is the reason for the state's existence. This is clearest in the *Republic*—which remains striking as a *political* treatise because it lacks a discussion of law—where the best state is governed by wise men who "know" the good, and who therefore must not be restricted in their commands and decisions. It is these philosopher-kings themselves, together with an educated citizenry, that for Plato hold the state together, not the impersonal bonds of law.

In open disagreement with Plato, Aristotle argues emphatically that a "government by laws" was superior to "government by men." Plato's preference for personal rule perhaps reflected a confusion of power in this world with power in the next. On earth, Aristotle wrote, power is never free of appetite and passion; even high spirits can pervert the judgment of office-holders, no matter how good they are. To be sure, laws must be wisely *implemented* by the government of men in all cases where the law, because of its general character, cannot lay down precise rules. But in an arresting sentence, Aristotle writes that to make law supreme in political life is to be regarded "as commanding that God and reason should rule; he who commands that a man should rule adds the character of the beast."[9]

In sum, it appears that both the "absolutist" and "legalist" theories contain truth about the nature of political power.[10] Both theories can be attributed to Paul without doing violence to his position in Romans 13. Both can be supported with other biblical texts. Advocates of either theory can turn to the history of biblical interpretation and discover entire periods when their theory was the preferred one. But neither theory follows necessarily from Romans 13. As important as they are for applying this text and generally for guiding Christians in politics, they do not come from Paul. As a Pharisaic Christian might put it, they are part of the "traditions of the Fathers," i.e., of the oral law rather than the written law.

But why is Romans 13 so controversial in the modern period? There are at least two reasons. First, the text suggests, though it never explicitly states, an anti-democratic theory of power. In the familiar circular logic of democratic thought, we obey government ultimately because government obeys us. When it doesn't, we recognize a right to resist and change it. This conception of government might be called the populist or *ascending* theory, because power is understood to ascend from the broad base of a pyramid (the people) to its apex (the premier, sovereign, president).

Directly opposed to this is the hierocratic or *descending* theory of political authority and power. Here original power is located in a Supreme Being who, when the theory is influenced by Christianity, becomes identified with the God of Abraham, Isaac and Jacob. Thus in the fifth century St. Augustine wrote that God distributed the laws to humankind through the medium of kings. Again the metaphorical pyramid appears, but now all original power is located at its apex rather than its base. The people "below" have no power at all except what is delegated to them "from above." All officers are appointed "from above," not elected by popular assembly. The supreme officer is responsible only to God.

The descending thesis was dominant in Europe in the Middle Ages; but since the recovery of Aristotle by Thomas Aquinas, and particularly since the Renaissance and the rise of liberal democracies, it has receded into the background. In the West, few remnants remain, though the economist Heilbroner foresees its return in post-industrial societies.[11] One reason why Romans 13 is controversial today is that it reflects this theory perfectly. In fact, the passage was an essential plank in all Christian versions of the thesis in the Middle Ages. Now that the theory is practically extinct, many Christians wish the *text* were also! A deep modern objection to Romans 13, in a word, is not religious or theological at all, but cultural. It is a political embarrassment with the stature of Holy Writ.

Also, the text remains controversial because it continues to be challenged by the same forces that led Paul to write it in the first place. If my thesis here is correct—that the New Testament harbors an abiding and perhaps justified suspicion of political life—we should not be surprised that it continually generates efforts to depoliticize its own most political text. Contemporary Christian exegesis of Romans is peppered with such attempts.

For example, in his otherwise helpful article "A New Theological Approach to Social Ethics,"[12] Hans-Werner Bartsch argues that Romans 13:1–7 should be "bracketed" in order to be correctly understood. First, its meaning must be qualified by the "eschatological bracket" of the waking and sleeping passage at the end of the chapter. Once "bracketed," the text loses its apparently establishmentarian force, and the deeper meaning of the first seven verses may be summarized thus:

1. "Governing authorities" in the text are revealed to be forces that still exist but whose power "in reality" is broken.
2. The passage does not attribute a peculiar "position" or "commission" to the state.
3. Even in the hands of a pagan civil power, Christians are not beyond the reach of the goodness of God.

Bartsch is correct in asserting that the 13th chapter of Romans is all of a piece, but his "eschatological bracket" illuminates exactly nothing. If the risen Christ is now Lord over all principalities so that their power, while still existing, is in principle broken, what are the implications for personal behavior, civic obligation, and the social use of power? Paul was deeply concerned with precisely these questions, and the beginning of an answer to them is to be found right in the text. No "brackets" are necessary. On personal behavior, "let us conduct ourselves becomingly . . . not in quarreling and jealousy" (v. 13); on civic obligation, "Let every person be subject to the governing authorities . . ." (v. 1). As we have seen, the passage does indeed attribute a peculiar dignity and commission to government. The fact that existing governments were pagan at the time Paul was writing is irrelevant if the text is political theory (about government *qua* government). Dozens of other passages in both Testaments (Romans 8 is among the most forceful) assure believers that they are never beyond God's reach; surely Christians don't need Romans 13 to learn *that.*

Bartsch's anti-institutional agenda is even clearer when he "brackets" Romans 13:1–7 with the love commandment in 12:1ff. and 13:8. This is a technique often applied in pacifist exegesis. Paul's use of the ultimate commandment to love one's neighbor, Bartsch writes, qualifies and restricts the demand to "be subject." So we must now ask: Do the regulations of government serve one's neighbor? Do I, through my obedience, rightly attest the love of God? Bartsch is asking important ethical questions here, to be sure, but again it is difficult to see their immediate bearing on Romans 13:1–7. If he means that the function of government is moral and that its highest virtue is justice for all, this point is in the text and no brackets are needed. If he means that Christ's command to love is a more fundamental, comprehensive demand than to seek justice, he is right—though again the point is made more clearly elsewhere (for example, in Matthew 5–7). If he means that the love command places Christians beyond the authority of civil law and governments in principle, this interpretation contradicts the text and a hundred brackets will be insufficient.

Bartsch's concern that the text will be used out of context (as German Christians did in the 1930's) is a valid one, but in his work we witness a time-honored method for dealing with biblical embarrassments: christen them "obscure," and then interpret them through passages which are "clearer." Scripture interprets Scripture. The problem with the method in this case is that the embarrassing passage itself proves to be every bit as self-evident as the others used to explain it. It is not wise to make too little of Romans 13.

Neither is it wise to make too much of it. The mistake made by pacifists who abhor the controversial verses is often imitated by conservative Christians who celebrate them. The classic error of Christian pacifists does not lie in their politics. Their insights into the demonic side of political life are often stunning (as Yoder's *The Politics of Jesus* amply confirms), and their "absolutist" view of power and iconoclastic exposure of the temptations and hypocrisy in politics have great value.

On the contrary, the typical weakness in Christian pacifism is its biblicism: the assumption that the New Testament contains a philosophy adequate to the task of "following Jesus" into politics. The Old Testament (not a favorite of pacifists) is much more concerned with politics than the New, but even there a faithful reader with political interests needs ethical and philosophical considerations to complement exegesis. Prompting faith in God is the real agenda of biblical texts, and it is probably wrong to assume that the meaning of *any* of them is directly political.

This is true even of Romans 13. It contributes controlling ideas to Christian political theory, to be sure, but the passage's center is not so much civic obligation and political power as faith and divine providence. It is Paul's theological assessment of his experience of Roman citizenship: namely, that the God who raised Jesus is the

God of Abraham, Isaac and Jacob, continuing to rule history not only above and in spite of governments, but also—mysteriously—through them.

NOTES

1. This chapter is adapted from my "The Riddle of Romans 13," *Christian Century* (Sept. 15, 1976), pp. 758–61.

2. Dietrich Bonhoeffer, *Ethics,* pp. 332–39.

3. The irony is that Marxism today has become a greater opiate—in precisely Marx's sense—than Christianity ever was. Though his book bears some marks of a fanatic against his own past, Bernard-Henri Lévy's insights on this point are stunning: *Barbarism with a Human Face,* Holoch, tr. (New York, 1979), esp. Ch. 18.

4. A. P. d'Entrèves, *The Notion of the State* (Oxford, 1967), p. 184.

5. National socialism could conceivably develop anywhere, of course, but the use of the Confessing church as a model of Christian political obedience can be misleading. The capitulation of German religious institutions, labor unions, and political parties to the Third Reich, as well as the isolated and exemplary resistance here noted, reflects a number of factors peculiar to Germany and should be viewed in historical perspective. Since the Reformation, the ties between German churches and the various states in Germany had been unusually close and the seizure of church lands in the eighteenth century tightened the financial ties even further, turning Protestant as well as Catholic churches into veritable servants of the state. One irony in the immediate situation was the way growing ecumenical sympathies among German Protestant churches in the 1930's, and their interest in a more unified Christian community played right into Hitler's hands. To Pharisaic Christian eyes, the most striking biblical characteristic of official Nazi Christianity was not so much its reading of Romans 13 as its effort to revile and do away with the Old Testament. See Ernst C. Helmreich's historical survey, *The German Churches Under Hitler* (Detroit, 1979).

6. Jacques Ellul, *Violence: Reflections from a Christian Perspective,* Kings tr. (New York, 1969), p. 84, *passim.*

7. John Yoder, *The Politics of Jesus,* p. 202, fn. 10.

8. It is here, and not in Greek and Roman antiquity, that the real foundations of modern constitutionalism can be found. Augustine as well must be excluded from this list, because his negative conception of the state is Platonic politics in religious garb, reflecting his spiritual insight into the complete transcendence of true justice and into the providential character of

all power in this world. See Carl Friedrich's analysis in *Transcendent Justice*, Ch. 1.

9. Quoted in d'Entrèves, *op. cit.*, p. 71. We here scratch the surface of a complex conflict of ideas which recurs continually in the development of Western political theory. My position is deeply indebted to this splendid book by Alexander d'Entrèves.

10. Cf. the recent discussions between Anabaptist and Reformed communities on political questions, as reported by Richard Mouw in *Politics and the Biblical Drama,* pp. 98–116. I agree completely with his conclusion (p. 116): "If Reformed Christians, and their political fellow-travelers among the faithful, are going to emphasize the legitimacy of political involvement in political structures, it must be with an Anabaptist-type conviction that the Christian disciple must walk in a new and better way."

11. Robert Heilbroner, *An Inquiry into the Human Prospect,* Chs. 4–5.

12. John C. Bennett, ed., *Christian Social Ethics in a Changing World* (New York, 1966), pp. 59–77.

V

THE LAW OF PEACE

You shall not kill.
Exodus 20:13

Pilate entered the praetorium again and called Jesus, and said
to him, "Are you the King of the Jews?" Jesus answered, "Do
you say this of your own accord, or did others say it to you
about me?" Pilate answered, "Am I a Jew? Your own nation
and the chief priests have handed you over to me; what have
you done?" Jesus answered, "My kingship is not of this world;
if my kingship were of this world, my servants would fight,
that I might not be handed over to the Jews; but my kingship
is not from the world." Pilate said to him, "So you are a
king?" Jesus answered, "You say that I am a king. For this I
was born, and for this I have come into the world, to bear witness to the truth. Everyone who is of the truth hears my
voice." Pilate said to him, "What is truth?"

John 18:33–38

"Law," wrote Thomas Aquinas, "is a rule or measure of acts,
whereby man is induced to act or restrained from acting."[1] Such a
definition represents nicely that extension of the concept of law
which is a legacy of both medieval and modern natural law theory to
legal philosophy in our time. Thomas is saying that law is *more than
command*. It does something else, and this something else does not
require the context of a superior and an inferior. Law teaches; it illuminates a particular quality of action. To natural law theorists, law is
"a standard . . . from which the quality of a particular action, the rel-

69

evance of certain situations and facts can be inferred . . . it is a logical
as well as a practical proposition."[2] This means that a law with no
apparent authority of a particular legislator or commander behind it
may yet be law. And conversely (as the "legalist" view of power con-
tends), a command carrying a superior's authority may *not* properly
be law.

Some such "extension" is necessary to counter the popular contention of legal positivism that morality is in no respect a determi-
nant of law, and in particular the apparently innocuous belief that all
law is legislation or the product of the will of a legislator. This belief
is anything but innocuous, of course; it stands the ancient function of
law on its head. The historical vocation of law has been to protect
people against tyranny and the arbitrary use of power. Positivism in-
sists that law actually includes any and every expression of the legislator's will. Law's essence is identified with its form; the law's
content can no longer help us distinguish between legitimate and illegitimate laws. Every state is a legal state; justice has nothing to do
with it. In the words of positivist philosopher Hans Kelsen, "just is
only another word for legal or legitimate."[3] Thus the drift of legal
positivism is to deliver law right into the hands of the power it is
meant to check: arbitrary government.

In fact, law is older than legislation. The sciences of ethology
and cultural anthropology are teaching us that law existed for ages
before it occurred to man that he could make or alter it. The notion
that man in his wisdom has designed the whole system of legal and
moral rights is not only dangerous but false; it is rooted in an intentionalist fallacy, and is normally marked by not a little intellectual
presumption.[4] It is certainly false if we define law in accordance with
Pharisaic Christianity: the intentional and behavioral shape of the
way of God. But it remains false even if we give to law the common
definition of enforced rules of conduct. There has never been a society without a modicum of social harmony and justice; and long before man developed language sufficient to issue commands, the
observance of common rules was what made social groups possible.[5]

Only as this intentionalist fallacy is laid aside can we see clearly
what has always been the case, that an essential purpose of law is
peace. "In its beginnings," notes legal philosopher Roscoe Pound,
"law [in the lawyer's sense] had for its end, and its sole end, to keep

the peace."[6] In an increasingly militarized society, the biblical law of peace directs the Christian community to contribute to this noble end in a distinctive way. Christians are to become God's peace movement, makers of peace in the name of its Prince. Let us see how.

The closer one looks, the more obvious it becomes that the word "peace" in the Bible (*shalom* in Hebrew, *irēnē* in Greek) suggests a reality of extraordinary depth and complexity. In the Old Testament, peace is understood as a divine gift; it is everywhere linked to the presence of God and his covenant. It is a feature of the relation between God and his people, particularly that confidence among the faithful that God's gracious presence in the midst of them will never end (Ezekiel 37:26-28). At the same time, the effects and range of this gift are breathtaking. No separation is suggested between "religious peace" of the soul and "secular peace" of protection against one's enemies, order and justice in economic life, and the like (Leviticus 26:3-13). Such a dualistic view of peace is unbiblical; its typical ideological function is to support a certain religious distaste both for the ambiguities of politics and for a morality of obedience in *all* realms of life.[7]

It is all too easy to become sentimental about peace, but fortunately the candor and integrity of the Old Testament writers will not allow it. The record they kept of Israel's past reminds each reader of the degree to which the history of mankind coincides with the history of armed aggression and war. Peace is something to be *hoped and prayed for* (Psalm 122), and is associated with the hope for a Messiah who will be its Prince (Isaiah 9). Some of Jeremiah's most scathing indictments are reserved for priests and prophets who, greedy for unjust gain, confuse the people by identifying periods of national tranquility with the peace of God (Jeremiah 6:13-14). Since genuine peace comes from God, "peace" without righteousness is a chimera. On the other hand, true righteousness will have peace as its effect (Isaiah 32:17). Purity and peace are inseparable. The salvation of God will be at hand when "steadfast love and faithfulness meet; righteousness and peace will kiss each other" (Psalm 85:10).

In the New Testament, peace refers on occasion simply to the absence of strife or war (Luke 14:32; Acts 12:20), its common meaning in classical Greek. But as in the Old Testament, it ordinarily is a theological concept. Jesus is himself the peace of his followers, because he unifies them in the Spirit, breaking down the walls of hostility between them; and because through Christ and his cross there is communion with God the Father, "bringing the hostility to an end" (Ephesians 2:14–18). Peace is part of the protective armor of Christians as they stand firm with the victorious Christ against the wiles of the evil one (Ephesians 6). The Johannine tradition stresses that the peace brought by Jesus is different from the peace the world gives (John 14:27), and cannot be achieved in the world at all apart from him. After comparing his relation to his disciples to a vine and its branches, Jesus alerts them that he will soon return to his Father, and bids them farewell:

> The hour is coming . . . when you will be scattered . . . and will leave me alone; yet I am not alone, for the Father is with me. I have said this to you, that in me you may have peace. In the world you have tribulation; but be of good cheer, I have overcome the world (John 16:32–33).

Given the richness and range of the concept of peace in Scripture, it shouldn't surprise anyone that there is no single biblical strategy for attaining it. Historically, Christians have quite properly endorsed a variety of political strategies for containing and reducing violence. However, the biblical law of peace suggests that certain common characteristics should mark *all* forms of Christian peacemaking. In the first place, the canon in its entirety should be consulted. Christians should attend carefully to the biblical law of government in their peacemaking, and criticize any peace strategy based on a form of anarchism contravened by Romans 13. In addition, they should be wary of those venerable, anti-political tendencies toward withdrawal and fanaticism rooted in the Christian movement itself (see above, Chapter 4).

These twin temptations, identified by Paul as "sleep" and "drunkenness" (1 Thessalonians 5), are doubtless aggravated by the peculiar position of Christian churches in the twentieth century. On the one hand, the spread of the Gospel in the last few centuries to the four corners of the globe had been remarkable. It testifies to the explosive missionary power of the Christian faith and its capacity to rise above particular cultural forms. Yet at the same time, Christians in the West are experiencing a wrenching erosion of their agency and social power. As Herbert Butterfield reminds us, just as Christianity lost its "Constantianian" predominance in European society deriving from an alliance with secular power, so Western man today—faced with the resurgence of Islam, the awakening of Asian and African peoples, and the rise of communism—is losing that easy primacy which he once seemed to possess everywhere in the world.[8]

It is therefore to be expected that Western Christians will be tempted to vacillate between a sleepy pessimism and a drunken triumphalism, both of which are induced by the same basic hankering after more comfortable days when the herd-spirit and custom and the authority of government were all on the side of the Christian religion. The pessimism will paint our century in much darker colors than it deserves, and commend a type of monastic option as the true way of peace. Much more dangerous—potentially at least—is the temptation to triumphalism. One of its milder forms is the Christian moral "crusade" against particular worldly evils such as drinking or the arms race. These efforts have often elevated public consciousness; but it is difficult to resist Bonhoeffer's conclusion that their impact in the long run is, at best, ambiguous.[9]

As in the Middle Ages, however, the Christian crusade can take a form that is not at all mild: the blessing of violence (national or revolutionary) as a means of attaining "peace with justice." In his history of Christian attitudes toward violence, Roland Bainton notes with approval that during World War II, the self-confident crusading mentality was absent from church social pronouncements, and has been moribund ever since.[10] Bainton was writing during the late 1950's, when the crusade may have been sleeping—but with one eye open. It lives on today in overly politicized theologies of the right ("Christian" anti-communism) and of the left (certain "theologies of revolution").[11]

Three recurrent characteristics mark the Christian crusade and help us identify it. The first is the moralization of conflict: our side is good, the other evil, no ambiguity. Second, there is a persistent tendency to demonize the enemy. Turning one's opponents into enemies "of God" or "of freedom" or "of justice" obscures the need to forgive and be forgiven, destroys one's sense of proportion, and sharply reduces the possibilities for compromise. Third, crusaders typically believe in the moral efficacy of violence.

The belief that fundamental progress can be secured through violence is a fascinating, attractive myth, a superstition. This is not to say that the hungry and the oppressed of the world do not have every right and cause to believe this superstition and act on it as well; nor does it mean that there are no circumstances where Christians should be encouraged to support *them*. What is meant here is simply that from the standpoint of Christianity, the belief is false. It contradicts the biblical law of peace, the structure of which may be suggested in the following three propositions:

1. To follow its Lord, the church must love its enemies.

The first thing Christ asks of his followers is never veneration but obedience, and this first proposition (Matthew 5:43–48) is one of his clearest commands. From a political viewpoint, it is also an otherworldly command, standing as a perpetual reminder of one of the ways in which the Christian community is called out from the world of everyday political life. A clear consciousness of the distinction between the church and the world is essential here. Note, in this connection, the care and sensitivity with which Jesus speaks to Pilate (John 18). To a politician unacquainted with Jesus' world-transforming message, his Kingdom is inevitably "not of this world." Were God's Kingdom of this world, Jesus tells Pilate, "my servants would fight"; for he is indeed King of the Jews, and injustice is being done by Annas, the high priest Caiaphas, and later by Pilate himself.

In political categories, the command to "love your enemies" is a *utopian* principle. No one should be surprised that it appears in perhaps the most famous utopian novel in recent years, *Walden Two* (1948). Through his mouthpiece, Frazier, B. F. Skinner sees the command as a technique of self-control, liberating all who use it from the inner devastation caused by anger at oppressive circumstances. Rather than hating your enemies, Frazier's Jesus teaches, practice the opposite emotion.[12] The problem with this interpretation is rooted in an aspect of Skinner's thought as a whole—his abundant, armchair faith in "behavioral science," a confidence based squarely on the premise that all obstacles to loving one's enemies are located in the environment and none in the self. To Pharisaic Christian eyes, *Walden Two* is insightful but finally frivolous, wish-full thinking, marked especially by a perfectibilist dismissal of the lessons of history and politics. This is why without a word about divine help, loving one's enemies appears so *possible* in Skinner's imaginative community. The apolitical character of the book's theme is not disguised.[13]

An otherwordly and utopian principle, "love your enemies" is also among the most profound and spiritually penetrating commands recorded in Scripture. As Paul Minear writes, we are here in the realm of "the mysterious junctions between God's importunate purposes and man's ambiguous and deceptive motives."[14] It is a call to Christian communities to continually examine themselves and their conflicts, for Christians are constantly tempted to fight evil in the manner of the world, and not after the manner of Christ. The real, fateful battle takes place on a different plane from our struggles with villains in the Kremlin, Havana, the Pentagon, or Teheran. "We fight not against flesh and blood," writes Paul, "but against the principalities, against the powers" (Ephesians 6:12)—not against political parties or nations, but against systems of evil deeper and more pervasive then any state. The decisive struggle in this world is with what the sophisticated historian Butterfield calls, without embarrassment, "daemonic forces."

> The daemonic forces against which we really have to fight are the ones which underlie Communism, Fascism, Nazism, atrocities in Palestine, and those curses of totalitarian war which the western democracies themselves have not avoided. They underlie these various evils precisely in respect of the features which are common to the whole series of them. The terrifying character of the evils lies in the things that they have in common.[15]

The temptation is so strong in this world to politicize or project into politics what is ultimately a spiritual battle that the capacity of even faithful Christians to resist it is gravely limited. Christian pacifism, therefore, has always been as much a witness to other Christians as to the world. The consequences of loving one's enemies is most evident in pacifist communities. The apparent ultimacy of political conflicts and promises is demythologized, and the tendency to demonize political enemies is checked and reduced.[16] The radical edge of the Great Commandment to love one's neighbors equally is perhaps honored *only* here, where "love your enemies" is more than a text read occasionally during worship.

2. To follow its Lord, the church should categorically reject the crusading option.

Once again, this proposition is directed only to Christians. Outside the Christian community, it will either make little sense or make sense for the wrong reasons. Unlike the just war theory, which is meant to guide those subject to overt enemy attacks, the crusading option is the advocacy by Christians of offensive violence in response to some sort of "systemic violence" or oppression. To reject this option is to invite a criticism which many genuine revolutionaries have long suspected, that Christianity is counter-revolutionary in principle. Though one might debate the meaning of revolution, there is clearly a sense in which these revolutionaries are right: Christianity is not politically ecumenical. Ellul has noted that Christian crusaders harbor a deep ambivalence about reconciliation as a dimension of Christian ministry;[17] and well they should, for it is precisely the reconciliation of *all* men and women in Christ that is assigned to outer darkness the moment one of Christ's followers wields the crusading option against his enemies.

A defense of this second proposition could move along at least three lines. The first is to examine carefully the political dimension of the life of Jesus, particularly the tension between Jesus and the Zealots. The ethical position of Pharisaic Christianity, remember, is that Jesus is the new Torah; his life and teachings integrate and radically fulfill all the commands of the Law (cf. Matthew 5:17). Jesus defines a way to live that is alternative to the ways of the world, and it is a way of peace. Pacifists have always been right about this. The heart of Christ's pacifism is not the fatalistic acceptance of political impotence, but rather the rejection of what John Yoder calls the "Zealot option," or the attempt through violent means to join God in the government of history.[18] It remains surprising and relevant that God's only Son considered others better than himself, and did not count equality with God a thing to be grasped (Philippians 2).

A second line of defense would be to consider once more Jacques Ellul's analysis of the nature of violence.[19] Ellul believes, correctly, that an essential requirement of Christians regarding violence is to perceive exactly what it is. When they put their textbooks and idealistic spectacles aside, he argues, Christians will see that even the most progressive societies are riddled with violence. Worse, history teaches that resorting to it is like playing with fire. To "use" it is in fact to be used by it, for violence operates *in every case* according to five iron laws. It becomes habitual; it spreads, prompting violent responses; it leads to condoning other kinds of violence; it begets lies and hypocrisy; and it is attended by continuous attempts to justify itself. In sum, "violence is hubris, fury, madness. There is no such thing as major and minor violence. Violence is a single thing and it is always the same."[20]

A third defense would be to learn from the political history of modern Western societies, particularly from what is perhaps its most alarming lesson: that nothing corrupts quite as swiftly and completely as the use of violence for idealistic purposes. We need look no further than the rise of fascism in Europe. It is a sentimental and gross simplification to believe that the crimes of fascist and communist governments in this century were authorized by appeals solely to the worst instincts in human nature. I know not a shred of evidence for this. On the contrary, Hitler, Mussolini and Stalin appealed also and often primarily to the highest ideals of justice for the downtrodden, national purpose, a higher living standard for all, and freedom.[21] They appealed, in a word, to the same ideals that guide not only terrorist organizations worldwide; they are the feelings that dominate contemporary democracies as well.

To reject the crusading option is not to reject revolutionary violence in every case. As Rich Mouw has written, mainline churches have been on the one hand too quick to approve of military campaigns *between* nations, and on the other too insensitive to the plight of oppressed peoples that prompts violence *within* nations.[22] Established governments are not always legitimate ones, nor are revolutionary groups always illegitimate. This is a political problem. The Bible does not resolve the tricky question of legitimacy.

3. To follow its Lord, the church should support the extension of the rule of law within and between states.

On the theological spectrum within the Christian faith, Pharisaic Christianity is probably in the best position to discern that the true vocation of the law is peace (cf. Psalm 119:165). It has always been true that law is the necessary companion of peace on this earth, as it is of genuine freedom. But this is particularly the case today. When a nation-state can inflict millions of casualties elsewhere in little over an hour, peace has become a moral imperative as never before in history. Loving one's enemies, however, does not magically transform them into friends. Advocating peace without extending the rule of law, i.e., without protecting the weak from aggression, is to walk away from the profound challenge of real peacemaking. Whenever peace becomes the *sole* objective of policy, a wise statesman has written, "the fear of war becomes a weapon in the hands of the most ruthless; it produces moral disarmament."[23]

Peace and justice must be sought together, or not at all. In the twentieth century, anyone not desiring an end to war is mad. All peacemaking stems from the desire, but the mission of the peacemaker is more difficult and complex: to end war without tempting the growth of tyranny.

These three propositions reflect well the type of Christian social action and moral leadership with which Pharisaic Christians are most comfortable. From an ethical standpoint, the primary task of the Christian community is seen as *being* something special, God's leaven in society, an anticipation of the Kingdom. The type of leadership stressed is clearly transforming rather than transactional. Transforming leadership seeks through example to lift the sight of one's community to action on a higher level. Transactional leadership aims at options currently and more or less conventionally available in a social system, obtaining results by exchanging one thing for another. As James Wall notes, liberal Christian churches have spent a great deal of energy in recent years in transactional leadership, working with secular allies and lobbying for specific political programs; and much real progress has resulted.[24] But now may be the time to give some attention to a distinct type of transformational leadership, which attempts to elevate public consciousness by intensifying and following biblical law.

In sum, only if peace were a less intricate reality could one commend a single Christian strategy for attaining it. Scripture licenses a number of approaches to peacemaking. A threefold summary of these strategies can be found in the work of Reinhold Niebuhr, who derives each of them from a particular way in which the Kingdom of God impinges on this world. Sometimes the law of peace must be obeyed in defiance of the world, though obedience means martyrdom and crucifixion. Without the *martyr,* Christians might forget that there is a contradiction between the Kingdom of God and the kingdom of the world. Sometimes the courageous obedience of a *prophet* is successful, forcing the evil of the world to yield, and thereby making a newer and higher justice in history possible. Human history is not completely tragic, but faces actual and realizable higher possibilities. However, sometimes force must be used to correct the injustices of power. Without the *statesman,* "we might allow the vision of Christ to become a luxury of those who can afford to acquiesce in present injustice because they do not suffer from it."[25] To the community that obeys biblical law—accepting the complexity, the risks, and potentially the suffering—the divine promise is clear:

O that you had hearkened to my commandments!
    Then your peace would have been like a river,
and your righteousness like the waves of the sea.

Isaiah 48:18

NOTES

1. Thomas Aquinas, *Treatise on Law* (Chicago, 1970), p. 3; *Summa Theologica,* Q. 90, ant. 1.

2. A. P. d'Entrèves, *Natural Law,* p. 78. Law in its widest sense, Richard Hooker wrote, incorporates teleology, for it is a rule by which work is done for an end: *Of the Laws of Ecclesiastical Polity,* Book I, p. 5.

80 · *Is Legalism A Heresy?*

3. Hans Kelsen, "The Pure Theory of Law," *Law Quarterly Review,* Vol. 50 (1934), p. 482. See Emil Brunner's remark, after watching the rise of national socialism in Europe: "The totalitarian state is simply and solely legal positivism in political practice": *Justice and the Social Order* (New York, 1945), p. 7.

4. See C. S. Lewis' telling attack on this presumption in educational philosophy: *The Abolition of Man* (New York, 1947).

5. This is still true today. See F. A. Hayek's *Law, Legislation and Liberty,* 3 vols. (London, 1973, 1976, 1979), particularly Vol. 2, Ch. 4, where he examines the anthropological evidence supporting the distinction between law and legislation.

6. Roscoe Pound, *Jurisprudence,* Vol. 1 (New York, 1959), p. 371.

7. This is the flaw in Edward Norman's controversial attack on the politicization of the World Council of Churches, and particularly on the ways in which Christian flirtations with Marxism lead to un-Christian obscurantism concerning the demands of the biblical law of peace. The strength of the book is Norman's critique of the W.C.C. view of the church, not his own alternative: *Christianity and the World Order* (London, 1979).

8. Herbert Butterfield, "The Prospect for Christianity," *Herbert Butterfield: Writings on Christianity and History,* C. T. McIntyre, ed. (New York, 1979), p. 252.

9. Dietrich Bonhoeffer, *Ethics,* p. 256.

10. Roland Bainton, *Christian Attitudes Toward War and Peace* (New York, 1960), pp. 221ff.

11. Jacques Ellul criticizes both types in *Violence,* Chs. 1–2.

12. B. F. Skinner, *Walden Two* (New York, 1948), p. 106.

13. *Ibid.,* pp. 193ff. *passim.*

14. Minear is referring to Christ's command to "watch and pray" (Mark 13:33) in his *The Commands of Christ* (Edinburgh, 1972), p. 177.

15. Herbert Butterfield, *Christianity in European History* (London, 1952) p. 57.

16. Skinner is alert to this: *Walden Two,* pp. 202ff.

17. Jacques Ellul, *Violence,* pp. 71ff.

18. John H. Yoder, *The Politics of Jesus,* Chs. 2, 5, 12.

19. See Ellul, *op. cit.,* Ch. 3. The irony of Ellul's book is that his attack on the crusading option is accompanied by a refusal to distinguish between violence and force, a refusal which undermines the coherence of any alternative position, save a strict pacifism that it is not at all clear he wants to embrace.

20. *Ibid.,* p. 99.

21. See Michael Polanyi's studies of modern ideologies in *The Logic of Liberty* (Chicago, 1951), pp. 93–110; *Personal Knowledge* (Chicago, 1958), pp. 228ff.

22. Richard J. Mouw, "Reversing a Pattern," *Reformed Journal* (February 1981), pp. 2–3.

23. Henry Kissinger, *White House Years* (Boston, 1979), p. 70.

24. James Wall, "The Fear of Piety," *Christian Century* (Sept. 19, 1979), pp. 875–76. The transforming/transactional distinction is drawn from this editorial as well; Wall derives it from James MacGregor Burns, *Leadership* (New York, 1978).

25. Reinhold Niebuhr, *Beyond Tragedy* (New York, 1937), pp. 285–86.

VI

THE LAW OF THE FAMILY

Honor your father and mother, that your days may be long in
the land which the Lord your God gives you.

Exodus 20:12

A woman in the crowd raised her voice and said to him [Je-
sus], "Blessed is the womb that bore you, and the breasts that
you sucked!" But he said, "Blessed rather are those who hear
the word of God and keep it."

Luke 11:27–28

The biblical law of the family strikes near the heart of a most
serious dilemma facing Christianity in the modern world. The natural family is among the most resilient of our institutions; yet in high-
ly mobile, industrializing societies, an insistent atomistic individual-
ism has been corroding the family structure for over two hundred
years now, and signs of familiar disintegration—from the divorce
rate to the abortion rate—surround us. The family has been steadily
losing its form and its social significance, which spells trouble. For
all its weaknesses, the natural family is the keystone of every civilized society, a bastion of human privacy and individuality. From the
ancient sages of Confucian China to the Islamic socialist Colonel
Qaddafi of Libya, the message is the same: a society failing to protect
and honor its families is a society in considerable danger.

For its part, the Bible is incontrovertibly—and to some femi-
nists, notoriously—supportive of the traditional family structure.
The evidence of scriptural conservatism on this point is overwhelm-

ing. "Keep your father's commandment," children are told in Proverbs,

> and forsake not your mother's teaching.
> Bind them upon your heart always;
> tie them about your neck.
> When you walk, they will lead you;
> when you lie down, they will watch over you;
> and when you awake, they will talk with you.
>
> (Proverbs 6:20–22)

"Blessed is every one who fears the Lord, who walks in his ways," promises the Psalmist.

> Your wife will be like a fruitful vine
>   within your house;
> Your children will be like olive shoots
>   around your table.
> Lo, thus shall the man be blessed who
>   fears the Lord. . . .
> May you see your children's children.
>
> (Psalm 128:1, 3–4, 6)

The thrust of the entire Old Testament on the subject, especially the Psalms and Proverbs, is to place family life under the category of divine blessing. A blessing is a special gift of God; the Hebrews used the word to indicate that something had been revealed to them about the nature and origin of a phenomenon. To interpret family life as a blessing meant that it was essentially good and grounded in mystery; its growth and dissolution can be neither fully understood nor manipulated by man.

This celebration of the family reaches full flower in the New Testament, where Jesus, against the laxity of his time, demands a purity in marriage so austere that even his disciples were startled (Matthew 19), and categorically denies the validity of divorce (Mark 10; Luke 16). His entire theology could be described as a transfiguration of the family. Indeed, its most surprising and resounding New Testament affirmation lies behind this in the fact of the Incarnation: God decides to become man in a family. Nineteenth century fundamentalists tried to turn this upside down; it is actually the *humanity* of Christ that is stressed in the doctrine of the Virgin Birth.

The Christian law of the family is not simply continuous with Hebrew thought, however. Though it draws on that vigorous patriarchal tradition so perfectly expressed in the Old Testament, it is—in two respects, visible even in the primitive church—a unique creation, and has had a tremendous impact on Western civilization ever since. While the patriarchal family was originally the privilege of a ruling race or a patrician class, the Christian family was common to *every* class, even to slaves.[2]

The more important change was Christianity's claim that within marriage, sexual obligations are mutual (Ephesians 5). The husband belongs to the wife as completely as the wife to the husband. Marriage became a more personal relationship than had been possible under the patriarchal system. The social effect of this was to give the family unit status and independence over against the clan, the race, and other social powers outside itself.[3]

In this light, the logic behind the New Testament advocacy of monogamy and of strict mutual obligations in marriage and family life is straightforward, almost obvious. What the Bible commends is not an instrument for the subjugation of women; and modern anthropology has discredited romantic myths about primitive states of society marked by promiscuity and sexual communism that the family supposedly displaced through a destructive repression of "instincts."[4] Primitive societies were hardly liberal in any respect, least of all sexual relations. The evolutionary hypothesis has done us a disservice here. To view the biblical posture as merely one stage in a developmental process, or as a transparent rationalization for a male-oriented social structure, is to miss the point.

The biblical writers were for the most part interested in only two subjects: God, and the nature of faith in him. Their intent everywhere was to describe, commend and defend faith—a vision of God at work in the world, a disposition of our whole being toward him, trust in him, and the like. Long before it was rediscovered by Sigmund Freud, they knew of the intimate connection between religious faith and sexual life; the biblical preoccupation with sexual experience would make no sense if they didn't. Sexual desire must be sternly regulated and controlled, they were convinced, or else the whole personality could become intoxicated, dissolving faith. The *Confessions* of St. Augustine provides vivid illustrations here. It is not at all a question of prudishness, so-called Puritanism, or looking the other way. On the contrary, in contrast with most alternative approaches, the outstanding characteristic of the Bible on this topic is the absence of guarded language. The biblical writers knew exactly what they were doing.

They knew also of the link between the growth of this relation called faith and what goes on in a child's earliest years. In childhood, education is more than mere learning. Apparently it is here, usually before puberty, that a person's basic dispositions are fixed, forms of seeing shaped, and character molded. What grows into our basic vision of the authority and order of the world usually reflects the model presented by our parents. The focus of the biblical writers on family life, then, is not difficult to understand. If faith in God is faith in a being wiser and stronger than man, whose will is not identical with man's but on the contrary is to be obeyed, who creates and loves each unique individual—if all this is true, then to encourage faith certain models of family life commend themselves.

In a characteristically pungent article, Paul Ramsey notes the silence in the contemporary pulpit on the host of biblical texts bearing directly on family life and its awesome responsibilities. "It has been a long time since I heard a series of sermons on the Ten Commandments"—particularly on the commandment prohibiting adultery, with its implications for premarital relations; and on the fifth commandment, with its stress on filial piety.[5] Ramsey explains this strange silence as the result not only of the world's effect on the church, but also of a massive betrayal *within* the church. Quite so.

But we have yet to tell the whole story. To equate what has been stated thus far with the biblical view would be to propagate heresy in the classical sense. It would be presenting part of the truth as the whole truth. The biblical law of the family has another dimension, a utopian-eschatological element.[6]

The word "utopia" comes from two Greek words which literally mean "no place." Utopias are pictures or images of human fulfillment, based on human wishes, with no place in the present. But as in the case of Marx's picture of a classless society, utopias are visions of what isn't which are always critically related to existing conditions. The extraordinary historical potency of utopias stems from this, for the genius of utopian artists is to so fashion their vision that there always appears to be a *path toward it from the present*.[7] One of the most powerful of such images is the Judaic hope for an age when all government will be handed over to a child sent from God:

> And his name will be called "Wonderful Counsellor,
>   Mighty God, Everlasting Father, Prince of Peace."
> Of the increase of his government and of peace,
>   there will be no end. . . .
> He shall not judge by what his eyes see,
>   or decide by what his ears hear;
> But with righteousness he shall judge the poor,
>   and decide with equity for the meek of the earth. . . .
> The wolf shall dwell with the lamb,
>   and the leopard shall lie down with the kid,
> And the calf and the lion and the fatling together,
>   and a little child shall lead them.
>
>   (Isaiah 9:6–7; 11:3–4, 6)

The realism of Pharisaic Christianity does not lead to a rejection of utopia. The dismissal of utopian thinking is characteristic rather of Christian rationalism. As we have noted, Pharisaic Christianity is itself a type of ecclesiological perfectionism. Its thinking is based in the Old and New Testaments, which themselves contain utopian concepts of immense historical power. Furthermore, only a moribund realism would insist on the rejection of utopian thought; what realism properly entails is that utopian ideas be clearly *identified as utopian*.

The Pharisaic Christian response to any utopian idea should be to expose it and test it against the Torah. It is difficult to overestimate the importance of this approach, because utopias are not only among the most powerful and fruitful of political ideas. They are also the most confusing and dangerous of political notions. Though they generate hope and confidence in the human prospect, they tend to consistently misconstrue man's situation in history, obscuring human limitations and sin—not to speak of divine providence and grace.

And modern thought is drenched with utopianism. The notion of progress, for example, is deeply rooted in the thought and practice of almost all Westerners and those influenced by the West. It is a gradualist utopian idea, the belief that a universal law of progress pervades all of history and that life will become "better and better" in the future than it is in the present. This belief is particularly widespread in the United States, where it conduces to the Pelagian spirituality of Benjamin Franklin and Jonathan Livingston Seagull: salvation is the result of striving and effort. Paul Tillich detects the same concept in the English version of the angels' anthem at the birth of Jesus, where the biblical text "good will to men" is translated "to men of good will." He calls this translation "one of the most fantastic utopias I have ever encountered," for it reflects the belief that sooner or later many men of good will—usually including ourselves—will obtain permanent control of things and then peace on earth will come.[8]

Let us examine, first, a persistent, minority view on the family that appears outside biblical thought. Beginning with Plato and continuing into the modern period, a utopian-eschatological tradition has emerged which is radically critical of the natural family. At its heart is the conviction that the relation between the family and social order is almost always misconceived. The fundamental issue is not the responsibility of society for the disintegration of the family, but rather the responsibility of the family for the disintegration of society. Advocates of the natural family say, "Outside the family, children would never learn to love and be loved." The utopian tradition answers: "In the family, children are loved by and learn to love *people like themselves,* reinforcing racial prejudice, class hostility, and nationalism. Social disintegration will be checked not by supporting the family, but by abolishing it."

"Abolition of the family!" wrote Karl Marx and Frederick Engels in *The Communist Manifesto* (1847–48), perhaps the best-known representative statement of this tradition. "Even the most radical flare up at this infamous proposal of the Communists." But the families everyone defends are located in the middle class; modern industry is systematically destroying families in the working classes, and no one objects. Furthermore, the sacralization of the middle-class family masks the exploitation of women within it, leading Marx and Engels to ridicule the bourgeois charge that the Communists will introduce a community of women.

> He [the bourgeois] has not even a suspicion that the real point aimed at is to do away with the status of women as the mere instruments of production in society. . . . The communists have no need to introduce a community of women; it has existed almost from time immemorial. Our bourgeois, not content with having the wives and daughters of their proletarians at their disposal, not to speak of common prostitutes, take the greatest pleasure in seducing each other's wives. Bourgeois marriage is in reality a system of wives in common and thus, at the most, what the communists might possibly be reproached with is that they desire to introduce, in substitution for a hypocritically concealed, an openly legalized community of women. For the rest, it is self-evident that the abolition of the present system of production must bring with it the abolition of the community of women springing from that system, i.e., of prostitution both public and private.[9]

Hostility to the traditional family structure in actual operation and in its social effects is a posture that does not originate with Marx and Engels. It can be found in Plato's *Republic*. The Bible picks up this tradition and transforms it in a distinctive way. The anti-family dimension of the biblical position is represented best perhaps in the monastic tradition of Roman Catholicism, and in some contemporary mutations of monasticism such as the Shakers, the Mormons, the Unification Church of Reverend Moon, and the Children of God.

Again, the key category is blessing. In the ancient pre-Israelite conceptions of blessing, magic was the leading element. Blessing involved an alliance between certain men and superhuman forces. Essentially it was a religious technique for avoiding bad fortune and for managing the future. To have a marriage or a family "blessed" was a way of teaming up with the powers that determined the outcome of family life, of ensuring marital bliss, and of turning nasty relatives into nice ones; it was an effective hedge against disintegration or tragedy.

The Hebraic blessing stood and still does stand in grand and awesome opposition to this conception. It is contra-magical at its core. Emphasizing the break with ancient theory, the Old Testament speaks repeatedly (as in Psalm 128, referring to family life) of God pronouncing the blessing himself. We can note three implications of this idea.

In the first place, whenever family life is good, fulfilling, fruitful and "blessed," it is God who is behind it no matter what other causes appear to be ultimately effective. Human beings, therefore, have no final control over the success or failure of family life, for God's blessing is decisive here, and the God of whom the Hebrews speak is not at man's disposal (Job 38–42). Does the family that prays together stay together? Perhaps, but not *because they pray* together.

Second, though it may be the occasion for the most exalted moments of intimacy and brotherhood and equality, there is nothing sacred about the family *per se*. Its goodness and power are real but derivative, and its sacralization (placing it above searching criticism) must be everywhere resisted in the name of God.

Third, family does not describe an exclusive realm with its own powers and principalities. All of life, private and public, is of a piece. The attempt to divorce issues of family life from issues of social and political health is forced and usually fraudulent, for the God of the family and the God of the Hebrew prophets is the same God.

In the New Testament this side of the tradition is elaborated further. It is revealed there that the family is not the communal goal of life but a shadow of the goal. It is like the end, not itself the end. In the New Testament, the natural family is basically a *community of preparation,* preparation for a new community where blood and sex and social status are no longer the basis for communion. A new family, a *koinonia,* is now groaning in travail, struggling to be born (Romans 8). The entrance to *this* family, a community open to all the world, is the crucified Christ (John 10). In Jesus of Nazareth, said the apostle Paul, the end has come: in him there is neither Jew nor Greek, slave nor free, *male nor female* (Galatians 3:28).

This meant that some harsh things had to be said to those who wanted to hold on to the natural family as something more than preparation. The woman wishing to bless Mary's womb and breasts was one such person. The problem was and is that precisely those people who understand the deep significance of the family—that it is an arena of God's special grace—are most tempted to idolize it and invest it with independent significance. This is why Jesus was on occasion so sharply critical of it: "If anyone comes to me and does not hate his own father and mother and wife and children and brothers and sisters, yes, and even his own life, he cannot be my disciple" (Luke 14:26). When told that Mary and his brothers were trying to reach him, Jesus said, "My mother and my brothers are those who hear the word of God and do it" (Luke 8:21).

What are the social implications of this position? Since the biblical posture is marked by an eschatological tension, the implications are necessarily complex; to simplify the consequences is to risk distortion. That risk notwithstanding, I believe the social implications of the biblical law of the family can be summarized as a double negative or as a call to a double resistance.

1. There are no grounds whatever for sacralizing the family.

The Christian community should reflect carefully on the biblical refusal to sentimentalize family life or to place it above criticism. This is particularly important in circumstances where Christian families appear to be threatened and the temptation to sacralize is strong. The appearance of homosexuals organized to procure their rights provides one such circumstance. The emergence of "Moonies" and the Unification Church is another. Moon's theology is a blend of millennial Christianity and Confucianism, stressing the God-centered family as the basic unit of salvation, and implying that Christ has returned again to complete the divine-human family either through or in association with Moon himself.[10] Like other forms of heterodox sectarianism, it is a critique of conventional norms and structures (in this case, familial ones); and Christian condemnations of Moon may be prompted as much by fear and an uneasy conscience as by a concern for freedom and orthodoxy.

The power and limits of the family are revealed nicely in Mario Puzo's *The Godfather* (1969), where loyalty to the family structure is at once essential to survival and the continuing source of massive and unnecessary violence. In an otherwise profound section on the church in the modern world, *The Documents of Vatican II* contains repeated references to "the sanctity of family life" and to "the sacred bonds of the family."[11] Such language is understandable and regrettably imprecise. The impulse to sacralize the family—whether in these documents, or on "The Waltons"—must be constantly exposed and resisted.

2. There are no grounds whatever for hating the natural family.

As we have seen, Luke 14:26 ("If anyone comes to me and does not hate . . .") is best understood within the Bible as a whole, and not apart from it. The utopian dream of a "new family," so strong in socialism and in certain forms of Christianity, is often generated by a hatred for the matrix that has sustained and shaped the dreamer, and without which this same dreamer would never have survived. Such hatred always veers perilously close to self-hate, and flies in the face of the biblical understanding of Creation. The most common illusion in the dream (if we can so speak!) is the picture of a world *humans can create* where conventional family life, with all its pitfalls, is absent. What authorizes this picture? Certainly not the history of our planet; the dream is utopian. Though there is a picture of a transformed family in Scripture, it is quite a different image. The Bible sees the natural family as an arena of God's special grace, a structure which prefigures the end or goal of human life.

To promote policies which undermine the family as an institution is nothing less, then, than a kind of suicide. George Gilder made this point well, if a bit aggressively, in an explosive tract with the title, *Sexual Suicide* (1973).[12] When part of the book first appeared as an article in the prestigious journal, *Harper's* (July 1973), it prompted the largest mail response, pro and con, in the recent history of the magazine.

Gilder's view of the family is not too different from the biblical one: a mysterious matrix of sexual love, intercourse, marriage, conception, childbearing, and child-rearing. He argues that almost every social disorder—violence, drug and welfare addiction, crime—is connected with familial disintegration. Women's, gay and other liberation movements have attacked the traditional family on the assumption that it perpetuates differences they wish to eliminate. But the natural family not only perpetuates these differences between male and female roles and realms; it is *based* on them. To undermine their social-structural support—rewarding welfare payments regardless of familial role or employment, for example—is usually to undermine the family itself. This is why the liberationist cure is often worse than the problem it purports to solve.

One approach to familial reform consistent with our position could be termed "piecemeal social engineering."[13] Its distinctive feature is the rejection of the metaphysics of the social contract. The "piecemeal" reformer views the family not as one of the few social institutions we have consciously designed, but as one of the vast majority that have just "grown" as the result of a virtually infinite number of human actions and of divine providence. Though he has hopes for the family structure as a whole, he does not believe in redesigning it as a whole. His approach is to "tinker," making an adjustment in one part of the family, and then readjustments, carefully comparing results expected with results achieved, and always on the lookout for unexpected consequences.

The biblical law of the family calls men, women and children to become fathers and mothers, sons and daughters, and brothers and sisters under God. Interpreting and applying this law is complicated because of the eschatological tension at its heart. Typically, the tendency is to overlook its subtlety and embrace either its pro- or anti-family component. To use Luther's image, the problem is a little like trying to get a drunken peasant on a horse: you push him up on one side, and he falls off the other.

As the ancients said, there is a Scylla and a Charybdis. If the Scylla is emphasizing Creation and the past or present to the point of an idolatry and worship of the family, the Charybdis is emphasizing eschatology and the future to the point of Manichean dualism. The trick theologically is to affirm the natural family and the coming kingdom of God at the same time, without confusing them. It is to avoid rejecting the God of continuity for the God of discontinuity (as in some liberation theology), or vice versa. The dilemma is a false one. What must be rejected is both of these rejections in the name of the God who was *and* is *and* is to come.

NOTES

1. This chapter is adapted from my "Patricia Hearst/Tania and a Theology of the Family," *Reformed Journal* (September 1974), pp. 14–17.

2. This same gradual change took place in China where, under the influence of Confucianism, all classes acquired family institutions which were originally peculiar to the feudal nobility.

3. Christopher Dawson, *The Dynamics of World History* (New York, 1956), pp. 163–64.

4. I am here repeating Bronislaw Malinowski's critique of Freudian instinctualism. See Dawson, *op. cit.,* pp. 159f.

5. Paul Ramsey, "Do You Know Where Your Children Are?" *Theology Today* (April 1979), pp. 20–24.

6. The picture of a perfect time (eschatology) and of a perfect place (utopia) should be distinguished in biblical thought, but I do not believe that they must or should be separated. See Martin Buber, *Paths in Utopia,* Hull tr. (London, 1949), p. 8.

7. Those interested in the subject might consult Paul Tillich's excellent article, "The Political Meaning of Utopia," *Political Expectations* (New York, 1971), pp. 125–80.

8. *Ibid,* p. 140.

9. Karl Marx and Frederick Engels, "The Communist Manifesto," in *Karl Marx: Selected Works,* Vol. 1 (London, 1942), pp. 224–25.

10. Herbert Richardson, "A Brief Outline of Unification Theology," in *A Time for Consideration: A Scholarly Appraisal of the Unification Church,* M. Darrol Bryant and Herbert Richardson, eds. (New York, 1978), pp. 136–37. This entire book is a fascinating study of the relation between the *human* (not only "religious") anxiety about orthodoxy and myths sanctioning religious persecution.

11. Walter M. Abbott, ed., *The Documents of Vatican II,* Gallagher, tr. (London, 1965), pp. 250ff.

12. George Gilder, *Sexual Suicide* (New York, 1973).

13. This awkward but useful phrase comes from Karl R. Popper, who contrasts it with "utopian social engineering" in *The Poverty of Historicism,* second edition (London, 1960), pp. 64–70.

VII

THE LAW OF GENDER

> Although they knew God they did not honor him as God or
> give thanks to him, but they became futile in their thinking
> and their senseless minds were darkened. Claiming to be wise,
> they became fools, and exchanged the glory of the immortal
> God for images resembling mortal man or birds or animals or
> reptiles.... For this reason God gave them up to dishonor-
> able passions. Their women exchanged natural relations for
> unnatural, and the men likewise gave up natural relations
> with women and were consumed with passions for one an-
> other, men committing shameless acts with men and receiving
> in their own persons the due penalty for their error.
>
> Romans 1:21–23, 26–27

The Bible contains a well-known prescription about homosexuality, a law of gender. Homosexual practice is sinful, and to be
avoided. But note *how* the subject appears. It is not even mentioned
by Jesus or by the Hebrew prophets. Though all biblical references to
it are negative, only three of them refer to unmistakably homosexual
practice between consenting adults—Leviticus 18:22, Leviticus
20:13, Romans 1:26–27. And not one of these texts singles out homosexuality for special condemnation, but includes it as one item in a
much larger mosaic of moral ruin.

The biblical refusal to stress homosexual sin comports well with
the main conclusions of John Boswell's remarkable historical study,
Christianity, Social Tolerance, and Homosexuality (1980). Boswell
virtually destroys the conventional notion that social intolerance of
homosexuals in the West has been a natural outgrowth of Christian

teaching. On the contrary, in the early church "most influential Christian literature was moot on the issue," and those writers "who objected to physical expression of homosexual feelings generally did so on the basis of considerations unrelated to the teachings of Jesus or his early followers."[1] It is Boswell's judgment that through the fourteenth century at least, Christian theology as a whole reflected no particular bias against homosexuals as a *social group*.

Furthermore, Christians of the Law should remember that with respect to issues lacking prominence in Scripture, there is often a legitimate pluralism within the Christian community. Legal Christianity is not the only orthodox Christian posture. As Richard Lovelace has suggested, Christians who believe that active homosexual behavior is compatible with Christianity might consider joining a denomination which endorses this lifestyle, such as the Unitarian Church, or the Metropolitan Community Churches.[2]

Within Pharisaic Christianity itself, however, the law of gender holds. It is not true that Paul's teaching on homosexuality is as "culture-bound" as his views on slavery and on the role of women appear to be, and is thus dispensable. The homosexual case is quite different. The total biblical context includes the liberation of the slaves at the Jubilee, the example of Deborah and other women, etc. However, nowhere in Scripture is homosexual behavior commended; it is condemned each time it is mentioned. But what exactly does this biblical prescription mean, and how should it be applied today?

As we have noted, the biblical writers simply do not pay much attention to homosexual practice. When they do, they list it with other sins including greed, adultery, suppressing the truth, disobedience to parents, and so forth. What we face here is the *assumption* that homosexual behavior is sinful. Nowhere in the Bible do we find the point *argued,* or even *claimed;* it is assumed as self-evident. Why?

The presumption against homosexuality evident in the Bible and in most Christian churches is rooted in the biblical view of human sexuality in general.[3] As noted in Chapter 6, Scripture supports the traditional family structure. From Genesis onward, sexual union is placed in the context of heterosexual companionship and the formation of the family. In the diversity and complementarity of male and female, men and women, husbands and wives, God crowns creation with a relationship displaying a range of qualities that reflect his own nature (Genesis 1). According to Christ, enduring heterosexual marriage is God's intention for sexual intercourse (Matthew 19).

Human sin skews this plan, the Bible teaches, with the result that none of us, heterosexual or homosexual, fulfill perfectly God's intention for our sexuality. Even our ideas about sexuality are clouded by sin, and in need of correction through revelation, through the Torah. No matter how subtle or original the theological concept, it is finally subject to the rule of Scripture; no matter how creative the moral insight, it too must meet this objective test. And to the God of the Bible, nothing is more acceptable than obedience. In the words of the 1978 United Presbyterian Policy Statement:

> Behavior that is pleasing to God cannot simply be defined as that which pleases others or expresses our own strong needs or identity; it must flow out of faithful and loving obedience to God. Sin cannot simply be defined as behavior that is selfish or lustful. Many unselfish deeds ignore God's expressed intentions for our lives. Homosexual Christians who fail to recognize God's revealed intent for sexual behavior and who move outside God's will in this area of their lives may show many gifts and graces. They may evidence more grace than heterosexual believers who so readily stand in judgment over them. This does not mean that God approves their behavior in the area in which they are failing to be obedient.[4]

The presumption against homosexuality is based also in the distinctive way the Christian tradition defines the love of God. In Christian theology, the model for all genuine love is divine love (1 John 4); and divine love—to use Hugh Koops' coined term—is more "heteragapic" than homoerotic.[5] The love of God is directed toward the other; it is not directed toward self.

The heteragapic motif appears again and again in the biblical tradition. In the Exodus, God does not love his people because they are wise, or good, or strong, or lovable, for they are none of these things. They are "a rabble" (Numbers 11:14). God simply loves them, and remembers his promises to their ancestors (Deuteronomy

4:35–37). This is the significance of the persistent reminders to Israel, throughout the Law and the Prophets, that she had been a stranger herself in Egypt, and that God loved her *there* (Exodus 20:2; 22:21; Hosea (9:10, *inter alia*). The basis of Israel's obligation to love the "fatherless, the widow, and the sojourner" is her own experience as a stranger, and her insight into God's love for the other.

The same motif is elaborated with great moral power in the New Testament, where Jesus identifies himself with outcasts and commends all who can recognize this and still follow him: "I was a stranger and you welcomed me" (Matthew 25:35b). Jesus' interpretation of neighbor love is heteragapic, choosing an outsider, a Samaritan, to represent obedience to God's Law (Luke 10:29–37). In his much-controverted counsel to perfection in the Sermon on the Mount, Jesus calls his listeners to love the other as God loves the other, i.e., to love their enemies (Matthew 5:43–47).

A suspicion of homosexuality in particular and of homoeroticism (the tendency to be aroused by one similar to oneself) in general is a natural outgrowth of this position. A great biblical symbol for God's presence in history is the relationship between male and female (Genesis 1:26–27); perhaps only the heterosexual bond can image the reciprocity of two beings so united and yet so different. With this starting point, Paul asserts that homosexuality reflects a tragic inversion in which men and women worship the creature instead of the Creator (Romans 1:26–27). It is not God's wish for humanity.

A proper restatement of biblical law is important in most types of Christian ethics; it is crucial in Pharisaic Christianity. The law of gender is simple and straightforward. The condemnation of homosexual practice is the clear teaching of Scripture. Nothing is gained by making the prescription appear more subtle or complicated than it is. What *is* complicated is applying it,[6] particularly in a society where homosexuals are so often victimized by widespread prejudice that they may be among the "strangers" with whom Jesus identifies himself in Matthew 25. The United Presbyterian position, approved in May 1978, is suggestive at this point.

First, the Presbyterians refused to unlink the grace and mercy of God from biblical law, divine redemption from divine judgment, freedom in Christ from obedience to Christ. As we have seen, this refusal is characteristic of legal Christianity. The authoritative source of norms for authentic life, they write, is the living Word, Jesus Christ, "who in risen power transcends time and space and the limitations of our values, norms, and assumptions to confront, judge, and redeem us." Christ comes to make us whole, to redeem us out of our fallen state and restore us to the goodness proclaimed at creation. But "the prelude to this redemption is divine judgment." Our redemption as sexual beings

> is impossible without repentance. To claim that God's love for us removes divine judgment of us is to eliminate the essence of divine love and to exchange grace for romantic sentimentality. There is a necessary judgment in God's love—else it cannot redeem. It was this Christ who said to the woman in adultery, "Go and sin no more" (John 8:1–12).[7]

The heart of Pharisaic Christianity could be put in Bonhoeffer's terms: grace without law is cheap. A salvation that accepts all persons regardless of their response is not the Christian message; it is vacuous universalism. As I hope this book demonstrates, the implications of this legal position go far beyond the specific issue of homosexuality.

A second signal feature of the Presbyterian position is its sharp distinction between the church and the world. Their policy statement refuses *even to consider* new scientific data on homosexuality outside of "the context of our theological understanding of God's purpose for human life" and of the church's mission. The church is explicitly warned against building theological conclusions on the shifting sands of current scientific understanding or of Christian experience undisciplined by Scripture.

> New data and hypotheses . . . in secular disciplines cannot in themselves determine a shift in the church's posture on this issue. . . . Frequently the results of scientific inquiry are tentative and inconclusive, neutral in their theological implications, or even weighted with unspoken values and assumptions that are misleading against the background of

biblical faith. . . . To conclude that the Spirit contradicts in our experience what the Spirit clearly said in Scripture is to set Spirit against Spirit and to cut ourselves loose from any objective test to confirm that we are following God and not the spirits in our culture or our own fallible reason.[8]

Pitting the Christian church so dramatically against its culture involves a number of risks, for the Presbyterians in this case and for Pharisaic Christians generally.[9] Two recurring dangers are legalistic self-righteousness and a turn away from the world. The Presbyterians anticipate both of them, and reject both of them.

They give no support whatever to churches that reject homosexuals, that respond to them out of contempt, hatred, and fear ("homophobia"). The church must "welcome homosexual inquirers to its congregations. . . . The church is not a citadel for the morally perfect; it is a hospital for sinners."[10] As *any* of us affirms Jesus as Lord and our intention to follow him, we become members of Christ's Body and should never be excluded from Christ's church.

Turning to Christian public responsibility, the policy statement instructs Presbyterians to distinguish carefully between public and private morality. State and local governments should decriminalize *private* homosexual acts between consenting adults. Criminal law does properly regulate "some sexual conduct . . . to preserve public order and decency, and to protect citizens from public offense, personal injury and exploitation." But like private heterosexual acts, homosexual acts in private "involve none of these legitimate interests of society."[11] Furthermore, legal discrimination against persons on the basis of sexual orientation in employment, public accommodations, and housing should be opposed.

In sum, the time-honored distinction between rejecting sin while accepting the sinner has never been more crucial than in Christian ministry among homosexuals. To accept the sin would be to condone models of sexual behavior potentially injurious to families, and to create the distinct impression that Scripture is more a wax nose than a rule of faith and practice. To reject homosexuals as special sinners is to cut the law of gender adrift from the Great Commandment. For in the New Testament, the "neighbor" whom Christians are to love is neither sex specific nor sexual preference specific. Not only is compassion for homosexuals not forbidden by the Great Commandment; it is a mandate of Christ's Gospel.

NOTES

1. John Boswell, *Christianity, Social Tolerance, and Homosexuality* (Chicago, 1980), p. 333.

2. Richard F. Lovelace, "The Active Homosexual Lifestyle and the Church," *Church and Society* (May–June, 1977), p. 36.

3. A fine legal Christian elaboration of this view is Lewis Smedes' book, *Sex for Christians.*

4. "The Church and Homosexuality" (New York, 1978), p. 59.

5. Hugh A. Koops, "The Christian Suspicion of Homosexuality," *New Brunswick Seminary Newsletter* (March 1979), pp. 18f.

6. Note John Calvin's sensitivity to this distinction throughout his discussion of the law in *The Institutes of the Christian Religion,* J. T. McNeill, ed. (Philadelphia, 1960), Bk. II, Chs. 7–9.

7. "The Church and Homosexuality," p. 58.

8. *Ibid.,* pp. 57, 59.

9. H. Richard Niebuhr has summarized the dangers of sectarian dualism in *Christ and Culture* (New York, 1951), pp. 65–82.

10. "The Church and Homosexuality," p. 59.

11. *Ibid.,* p. 61.

VIII

THE LAW OF CONSUMPTION

And behold, one came up to him [Jesus], saying, "Teacher, what good deed must I do, to have eternal life?" and he said to him, "Why do you ask me about what is good? One there is who is good. If you would enter life, keep the commandments." He said to him, "Which?" And Jesus said, "You shall not kill, You shall not commit adultery, You shall not steal, You shall not bear false witness, Honor your father and mother, and, You shall love your neighbor as yourself." The young man said to him, "All these I have observed; What do I still lack?" Jesus said to him, "If you would be perfect, sell what you possess and give to the poor, and you will have treasure in heaven; and come, follow me." When the young man heard this he went away sorrowful; for he had great possessions. And Jesus said to his disciples, "Truly, I say to you, it will be hard for a rich man to enter the kingdom of heaven. Again I tell you, it is easier for a camel to go through the eye of a needle than for a rich man to enter the kingdom of God." When the disciples heard this, they were greatly astonished, saying, "Who then can be saved?" But Jesus looked at them and said to them, "With men this is impossible, but with God all things are possible."

Matthew 19:16–26

In legal Christianity, the proper ordering of the Christian community is seen as a prototype for the ordering of larger communities. As Barth has written, the church is "to represent the inner within the outer circle."[1] There are two sectors of our modern world where this distinctive witness of the church's own life has special moral urgency. The first sector, explored in Chapter 5, is the vocation of peacemaking in an increasingly violent and militarized society. The second is an economic one: to bring judgment and hope to a world where unprecedented affluence and consumption levels exist alongside massive poverty.

The biblical law of consumption guides the church between opposite heresies that continually tempt Christians in economic life.[2] One is to view the economic realm as a separate, secular sphere utterly distinct from the spiritual concerns of Christianity. The chaos, complexity, and gross inequities that exist in relations between the rich and the poor all provide incentives to embrace this view. But it is false, for it denies the reality of the Kingdom of God in history. Biblical Christianity does not leave Christians without guidance in their everyday economic decisions.

The other heresy is to identify some particular economic system with the will of God, and thereby place it beyond the reach of criticism. Religious conservatives are tempted to do this with capitalism, religious liberals with various forms of socialism. The essence of the heresy is to deny or obscure the eternal destiny of human beings, and to pretend that a particular socio-economic system can provide its members with what amounts to salvation.

But the true aim of the law of consumption is a constructive task inside the camp. Summarized in that disturbing story of the rich young ruler, its aim is the reformation of the economic life of the Christian church. Thus its appropriate impact on social change is at once indirect and substantial. For how can the economic reformation of a whole society be brought about if it is common knowledge that Christ's church itself is preoccupied with self-preservation or its own material privileges? In the words of the World Council of Churches' first social pronouncement, "The greatest contribution that the church can make to the renewal of society is for it to be renewed in its own life in faith and obedience to its Lord."[3]

It is a mistake to deduce any political view of property from the New Testament. Martin Hengel has shown that such a view does not reach definition there.[4] What we do find, in both the Old and New Testaments, is a *prophetic critique of riches* accompanied by a demand for radical detachment (from wealth) and for helping the less fortunate. "Woe to those," thunders Isaiah, "who decree iniquitous decrees . . . [who] turn aside the needy from justice, who rob the poor of my people of their right. . . . What will you do on the day of punishment . . .? To whom will you flee for help, and where will you leave your wealth?" (Isaiah 10).

"Do not lay up for yourselves treasures on earth," Jesus preaches, ". . . but lay up for yourselves treasures in heaven" (Matthew 6). In his encounter with the rich young ruler, Jesus gives further embodiment to this prophetic tradition. His command "Sell what you possess" is at once so explosive, so inspirational and so embarrassing that it raises the same question for us today that it did for Jesus' disciples and for Clement of Alexandria: Can a person with possessions be saved?

At the beginning of the third century, Clement delivered a sermon on this question, and it remains one of the best interpretations of the rich young ruler passage ever written. Clement had been watching Christians respond to Jesus' prophetic utterances, and saw some unexpected spiritual and social effects: hatred of the rich, self-hatred among the rich, exclusion of the rich from the church, fiscal chaos, etc. The sermon deals with the dangers of wealth, for this is what the passage is about. But the heart of the sermon lies elsewhere.[5] His essential subjects are the derailments possible when faithful wealthy Christians *hear Christ's teaching* in the passage, Christians who believe that (with God's help) to obey Jesus here is not impossible, and who refuse to focus this "counsel of perfection" only on Christians somewhere else. The three derailments Clement lists have continued to plague Christians since the third century. All three are alive and well in comfortable, prosperous churches today.

The derailments are despair, irrational moralism, and superstitious spiritualism. The first two, Clement argues, spring from a materialistic error about what exactly prompted the rich young ruler to depart from Jesus. The third confuses the cause of greed with its occasion, and "condemns wealth as a traitor and an enemy to life."[6]

There *is* a law for Christians in this passage, Clement writes, but its spirit must be stated with precision. The higher the law, the more it is true that "the written code kills" (2 Cor. 3:6). "Sell your possessions" is close to the mark but lends itself too easily to a secular, materialist reading. The law that convinced the young man to depart from Jesus might be put thus: "Sell what possesses you." It is this that the rich man could not bring himself to do. What Jesus required, in Clement's words, was that he "banish from his soul his notions about wealth, his excitement and morbid feeling about it, the anxieties, which are the thorns of existence, which choke the seed of life." It is a "lesson peculiar to the believer, and . . . instruction worthy of the Savior."[7]

Hearing Christ's command as "Sell your possessions" may lead to disappointment—when one discovers that there is nothing inherently noble about poverty, and that merely giving up things can leave pride, pretension and arrogance (Clement's "passions of the soul") all too firmly in place. More often, Clement argues, it leads to despair. Wealthy Christians conclude that they are not destined for the life to which Christ calls them. They inwardly turn away from Christ and surrender to the world, "clinging to the present life as if it alone were left to them."[8] Clement's insight is still on target: the death or diminution of Christian faith in the West can only fuel that acquisitive spirit already so prominent in parts of American society and Western Europe.

The second derailment is irrational moralism. Clement was concerned lest this controversial stricture from Jesus generate an ideology for dividing his church, particularly along class lines. One of his deepest convictions was that Christ's demand had universal reach. Like all words of Jesus, these were words of hope, and were addressed to every believer—not just to the clergy on some "higher way," and not only to Christians without means. But if this was the case, the passage had to be explained. Clement interpreted the story as judging wealth critically, but not ruling it out in principle. Stress was laid on its right use within the community, and on the renunciation of avarice and luxury.[9]

The third derailment is superstitious spiritualism. Here riches and possessions are *themselves* viewed as the source of greed, and Jesus is interpreted as commending a wholesale flight from them. In fact, Clement argues, such a position does not come from Scripture at all, but from a gnostic revulsion at the material world, a view which denies or obscures the goodness of Creation.[10] The message in the passage is not to cast wealth into the sea, but to use it "with wisdom and sobriety and piety" to benefit our neighbors. Surely the

Lord does not out of one side of his mouth require us to abandon property, and then out of the other enjoin us to use our property to give food to the hungry, water to the thirsty, and clothing to the naked![11]

As the lives of Christians are reformed by this law of consumption, so must be the Christian community as a whole. For individual Christians to sell what possesses them, they need the support and encouragement of a church that does the same thing. By God's grace, such churches can be leaven and salt within the structures of our economic life—communities resisting the spirits of this world, and anticipating the Kingdom of God. In a word, they bring the world judgment and hope, and have at least these three marks:

1. The Christian church should be a sphere of resistance to economic idols that possess us.

How much is enough? What is an appropriate level of consumption for followers of the God of righteousness and justice? These are not easy questions for American Christians, and for a fairly clear reason: the unprecedented and staggering level of resource consumption that now pervades every sector of American society. Even a poor person in America consumes more basic raw materials per day than the average person in Denmark, and more than the typical rich person of a century ago.[12]

The United States is a consumer society without precedent in the history of the world. At the same time, two-thirds of the world's population goes to bed hungry every night. High consumption levels in developed countries depend upon an intricate, massive resource procurement system with global reach. Whether Americans have "enough" is intimately related to the scarcity that faces people elsewhere in the world.

In this setting, the two crucial questions for American Christians have been posed recently by Richard Barnet.[13] First, is scarcity real? Is it true that there are just not enough goods to go around, or do modern economic and political systems create scarcity for some, or are both claims true? To what extent are the current gross imbalances in consumption levels *necessary*?

Second, how is the control over resources in the post-OPEC era changing and what does it mean? Rich and poor nations struggle continually over their share of the world product. The "energy crisis" in the West signaled a shift in power among those who control our resource systems. The question of who will control and benefit from future resource distribution bears not only on the prospects for justice but also on the making of peace. War has been a typical way for great nations to meet their resource needs. If there is another war, it will most likely be over what industrial nations are accustomed to regard as essential to survival.

Both these questions are crucial ones. Any ideology that diverts us from them or obscures them for American Christians can *ipso facto* be considered an economic idol bent on possession, and should be resisted. A most insightful analyst of economic idols in Western society is the liberation theologian Douglas Meeks. In a recent article, he notes three of them.[14]

The first is the spiritualization of work. Many of us have become convinced that we *are* what we do on the job. We are so afraid of scarcity and so compulsive about earning more (i.e., about *growth*), that work becomes the way we distinguish between people and the way we justify ourselves. What is sickness? Not being able to work. What is deviancy? Refusing to work. How are our high consumption levels justified? We work. How are high poverty and unemployment levels among blacks and Mexican Americans explained? They are lazy and refuse to work. Thus, spiritualized work "possesses" us, intensifying racism and hatred of the poor.

A second idol is the spiritualization of money and commodities. To want more has become a sign that we are alive. To possess or desire to possess certain products often is the motive and end of our existence. Thus our natural love of things is spiritualized, and becomes a mighty acquisitive engine fed by the fear of scarcity and the related need to get an ever greater share of the pie.

A third idol is the spiritualization of scarce goods within advanced consumer societies. Fred Hirsch calls these goods "positional," and they include top jobs, mobility, recreation, education, services and leisure. In his book *Social Limits to Growth,* Hirsch argues that the more the basic material needs of a population are met, the more intense becomes the competition for these positional goods, the very attractiveness of which *decreases* as more and more people gain access to them. The natural response is to keep making these goods more scarce by making them more expensive and more exclusive. Thus year by year the destructive competition for them increases, and our ability to truly live with and for one another in such societies decreases.[15]

2. The Christian church in the economic sphere should be a sign of hope, anticipating the kingdom of God.

One of the greater temptations facing Christians today is to give in to "apocalypse chic," a pessimism about our future that is on occasion all too rational. After all, the eventual slowing of industrialization in affluent nations is a probability. The population explosion continues, fueling famines and complicating the job of dividing the world's resources more justly. The proliferation of nuclear weapons raises the prospect of nuclear terrorism and of wars designed to acquire a fairer share of the earth's resources.

But Christians should not accept our corps of doomsday prophets uncritically. Their pessimism has become fashionable in some circles, and often contains a lively streak of melodrama. The Christian message is one of hope, not only in the world to come but in this world. For such hope to be announced and embodied only by individual Christians is not enough. The structure of Christian *churches* should reflect and support the hope Christians carry.

But how? Four years ago, evangelical Christian Ron Sider published a book entitled *Rich Christians in an Age of Hunger* which has since received an unusual amount of attention, even outside evangelical circles. The reason for this, I believe, is that his bracing thesis is incontestable: "Simpler living is a biblical imperative for contemporary Christians in affluent lands."[16] This is the key direction for prosperous churches as they forge faithful lifestyles for Christians in an age of hunger.

Part III of Sider's book bristles with practical suggestions for implementing his thesis. But he also states why the Christian *community* is so important to the process. The answer is "cognitive deviance." Christians are a cognitive minority in the secular West. In other words, their belief system differs sharply from the majority in their society. This is particularly true as Christians try to hold to the ethics of Jesus' kingdom within a consumption-oriented, materialistic culture. The successful maintenance of such an ethic requires the support of counter-communities with considerable vitality and strength.[17] If to be Christian is to lovingly defy the world, then Christian churches must become communities of loving defiance.

3. The Christian church should be a sign of hope in the world to come, anticipating the Kingdom of God.

Perhaps the greatest vocation of Christ's church has always been to announce the promise of "the resurrection of the body and the life everlasting." Here Christianity veers close to the ancient Pharisees. It was Paul's previous standing as a Pharisee that gave force to his question to Jews before King Agrippa: "Why is it thought incredible by any of you that God raises the dead?" (Acts 26:8). The present life is not all there is: the greatest hope is for eternal life.

This grand message in Christianity can be distorted. It can be used to divert the aspirations of distressed people away from justice in this world. It can obscure the realities of poverty and social injustice by its attention to the soul and to personal decision. The rise of communism in its modern totalitarian form is in part a prophetic judgment on orthodox Christian indifference to the plight of the lower classes. The message of heaven can be an opiate on earth.

But abuse does not contravene right use. Christian hope is distorted every bit as much by *too little* attention to the life to come as by too much. Over against a secular society, it would be surprising if some Christians didn't experience a certain failure of nerve on this point. One of the dimensions of "classical" Christian writing is the author's capacity to balance interest in this life with meditation on the life to come. Calvin's discussion of the Christian life, for example, is quite remarkable in this respect.[18]

Without this balance, the hope announced by Christianity will be misinterpreted. It can create utopian dreams, millenarian fantasies, and political chaos. This has particular significance for the economic sphere, since we live in a commercial civilization. The tradition of political realism has always been sensitive to the problem. There is no simple way of moving from the moral standards of love and sharing appropriate to individuals or to intimate associations such as the church, to the political behavior of social classes, nations and empires. Reinhold Niebuhr made this distinction a little too sharply in his first major book, but the point still holds.[19]

Christian hope for this world, which leavens the lives of the lost with a confidence no darkness can overcome, must itself be leavened by Christian hope in the future life. It is one thing to argue that Christianity has some definite things to say about economic and political problems, and quite another to claim that what it says solves any of them. "Who actually tells us," Bonhoeffer asks rhetorically, "that all worldly problems are to be and can be solved? Perhaps the unsolved state of these problems is of more importance to God than their solution, for it may serve to call attention to the fall of man and to divine redemption."[20]

The perfectionist impulse in politics, which Augustine detected throughout Greek and Roman classical thought, did not die when he refuted it.[21] It lives on today in myriad forms, some of them encouraged by Christianity. At its heart is the belief that a sort of salvation (permanent peace, security, and freedom) can be procured through political action. A central instinct of legal Christian realism is to deny this belief, because Christian realism is Augustinian. Salvation is even now, for Christ has come; but salvation is *not yet,* for Christ is coming again.

No model of the church in economic life is perfect or without potential problems. Our stress on the church's uniqueness carries with it the danger of sectarianism. Sectarianism is puritanism gone sour. The church is distinct from the world, but an aim of *Christian* non-conformity is a more inclusive embrace of the world's people. God's love falls like rain upon those who love him, but also on those who do not. Appropriately enough, we must beware of a certain "pharisaical" worldliness. Barth's warning is apt: "The church manifests a remarkable conformity to the world if concern for its purity and reputation forbid it to compromise itself with it."[22]

The church's solidarity with the world should be nowhere more evident than in the struggle for economic justice. Every individual on this earth is a child of God, and close to a half-billion of them are malnourished. You don't need a Bible to see the outrage in this. Though it helps, even the Christian religion is not necessary. The only thing required is a sense of justice.

> There is one thing, and one thing only, which defies all mutation; that which existed before the world and will survive the fabric of the world itself; I mean justice; that justice, which, emanating from the Divinity, has a place in the breast of everyone of us . . . and which will stand, after this globe is burnt to ashes, our advocate or accuser before the great judge. . . .[23]

NOTES

1. Karl Barth, *Community, State and Church* (New York, 1960), p. 186.

2. The twin heresy notion is drawn from the Oxford Conference Report (1937), an ecumenical Protestant document throughout which the influence of Reinhold Niebuhr can be discerned. Quoted in Waldo Beach and H. Richard Niebuhr, *Christian Ethics* second edition (New York, 1973), pp. 481–98.

3. W. A. Visser 't Hooft, ed., *The First Assembly of the World Council of Churches* (New York, 1949), p. 80.

4. Martin Hengel, *Property and Riches in the Early Church* (Philadelphia, 1974). "For the first Christians the question of property was a question of personal ethics or at most the problem of relatively small groups. . . . The possibility of better social legislation by the state was no more within their scope than the limitations of the economic omnipotence of the state": p. 85.

5. John Passmore's generally excellent analysis of Clement's sermon is flawed by the assumption that the Alexandrian was formulating a rule governing the possession of wealth *per se*. But he was not, and neither—I believe—was Jesus in this passage: *The Perfectibility of Man*, pp. 116–117.

6. Clement, "The Rich Man's Salvation," quoted in Beach and Niebuhr, *op. cit.*, p. 98.

7. *Ibid.*, pp. 94–95. To be renounced are precisely "those possessions that are injurious, not those that are capable of being serviceable": p. 97.

8. *Ibid.*

9. Clement's nightmare came true two centuries later when the British monk Pelagius, appalled by moral laxity in Rome, rejected the reasoning in Clement's sermon and taught that the wealthy cannot hope to be saved.

10. This same heresy is even more prominent in the gnostic view of birth, celibacy, and marriage. Clement attacks this as well in his "On Marriage" in *Alexandrian Christianity,* Oulton tr. (Philadelphia, 1954), pp. 40–92.

11. Beach and Niebuhr, *op. cit.,* pp. 96–97.

12. Marc Ross and Robert Williams, *Our Energy: Regaining Control* (New York, 1981), p. 5.

13. Richard Barnet, *The Lean Years* (New York, 1980), pp. 18–19.

14. M. Douglas Meeks, "The Holy Spirit and Human Needs," *Christianity and Crisis* (November 10, 1980), pp. 314–15.

15. Fred Hirsch, *Social Limits to Growth* (Cambridge, 1977).

16. Ronald J. Sider, *Rich Christians in an Age of Hunger* (Downers Grove, 1977), p. 188.

17. *Ibid.,* p. 192.

18. John Calvin, *The Institutes of the Christian Religion,* Book III, Chs. 6–10.

19. Reinhold Niebuhr, *Moral Man and Immoral Society* (New York, 1932).

20. Dietrich Bonhoeffer, *Ethics,* pp. 355–56. Jesus' famous remark, "You always have the poor with you" (Matthew 26:11), has similar force. Cf. Bruce Birch and Larry Rasmussen, *Bible and Ethics in the Christian Life,* pp. 179–82, where the authors so fear the otherworldly overtones in Jesus' comment that their interpretation of the passage turns the Savior into a social democrat.

21. A definitive study of this refutation is Charles N. Cochrane, *Christianity and Classical Culture* (New York, 1940).

22. Karl Barth, *Church Dogmatics,* IV/3, Pt. 2, p. 775.

23. The speaker is Edmund Burke, quoted by Carl Friedrich, *Transcendent Justice,* pp. 19–20.

IX

THE WEAKNESS OF
PHARISAIC CHRISTIANITY

He [Jesus] . . . told this parable to some who trusted in themselves that they were righteous and despised others: "Two
men went up into the temple to pray, one a Pharisee and the
other a tax collector. The Pharisee stood and prayed thus with
himself, 'God, I thank thee that I am not like other men, ex-
tortioners, unjust, adulterers, or even like this tax collector. I
fast twice a week and I give tithes of all that I get.' But the tax
collector, standing far off, would not even lift up his eyes to
heaven, but beat his breast, saying 'God, be merciful to me a
sinner!' I tell you, this man went down to his house justified
rather than the other; for everyone who exalts himself will be
humbled, but he who humbles himself will be exalted."

Luke 18:9–14

The song of Pharisaic Christianity is a significant theme in the
Christian chorus, though most Christians are likely to prefer other
parts. A good deal of its permanent value rests in the capacity to
challenge and criticize other types of Christianity. But only a glance
of Christian (especially Orthodox and Protestant) ethics over the last
fifty years is required to realize that the reverse is also the case. Even
in the New Testament, the harmony in the Christian "symphony" is
usually a good deal less than celestial; the Bible displays some of the
characteristics of debating society minutes. The weakness of Jewish
Christianity is exposed best in the sayings and writing of two Jews
with first-hand experience of Pharisaism: Jesus and Paul.

There is no evading biblical interpretation, for Scripture never fully interprets itself. The best an interpreter can do is to be as candid as possible about the hermeneutical (interpretative) principles used, and continually reform them in light of Scripture, tradition, and the promptings of the Holy Spirit. In addition, since every interpreter is a *social* being, it is a mistake to pretend that modern social problems have no bearing on hermeneutics. One of the heaviest burdens in all industrial, efficiency-oriented societies is the pressure to achieve something. The worst thing that can be said of anyone is that he has achieved nothing. Modern life pushes us to keep up our achievements, to provide evidence of our achievements, to justify ourselves by our achievements. In modern dress, this is exactly what Paul meant by "the curse of the law." Hans Küng is correct—in our Western social context—to warn against the stress on works over faith in the book of James, and to openly state his preference for Paul, particularly for Paul's profound attack on legalistic "justification by works."[1]

A hermeneutical principle underlying this book is that the target of the polemic against legalism in the New Testament was an abuse of the law model to which Jewish Christians were prone. Because Christian leaders were (and are) peculiarly tempted by this abuse, and because it usually hides behind a facade of righteousness and propriety, legalism was perceived early as a particularly dangerous (though far from the only) distortion of the Christian faith, a danger which can be measured by the force of the New Testament invective leveled against it. One of the lessons of history is that no Christian community is exempt from the peril of legalism, and Christians need to be continually reminded of its roots, masks, and consequences.

In his *Jesus and the Law in the Synoptic Tradition* (1975), Robert Banks notes that in both action and attitude, the Synoptic Jesus consistently takes up a position over against the Pharisees. This anti-Pharisaism is a mere by-product, however, of Jesus' primary concern, which is obedience to the mission to which he had been called. In the sabbath controversy (Matthew 12), in the disputes over divorce (Matthew 19) and defilement (Mark 7), in the antitheses of the Sermon on the Mount (Matthew 5–7) and elsewhere, Jesus demonstrates a sovereign freedom and transcendence over the demands of the Law. But it is not at all easy to identify the *way* Jesus transcends Law. Why? Because he never takes a clear position on the Law, a fact which alone is enough to distinguish Jesus sharply from the Pharisees.[2]

The unity in Jesus' position, Banks argues, rests in his consistent subordination of *halakic* questions (questions of lawful conduct) to his own messianic ministry, for Jesus' ministry—his teaching and practice culminating in the Cross—is itself the Law's "fulfillment" (Matthew 5:17). To be Messiah can mean no less. Banks concludes: "It is *to* that ministry that the Law 'prophetically' pointed, and it is only insofar as it has been taken up *into* that teaching and completely transformed that it lives on."[3] In each and every encounter between Jesus and the Pharisees portrayed in the Synoptics, the Pharisees cling to the Law so firmly that they don't recognize its fulfillment in a person. Their very allegiance to divine Law obscures the new age heralded by the appearance of God's Son. This is the error to which all legal Christians are subject. It is the cardinal Christological temptation of Jewish Christianity, and a heresy narrowly avoided in the book of James.

In his arguments with the Pharisees, the moral fault to which Jesus returns again and again is spiritual pride. Religious pride is a spectre haunting Christianity as a whole, of course, but it is particularly elusive and at the same time potentially virulent among Jewish Christians who stress ethics and right practice. It is not insignificant that when attacking this fault, Jesus on more than one occasion compares Pharisees with tax collectors, the despised Jewish collaborators with Roman oppression; and the Pharisees come off second-best. In the parable of the Pharisee and the publican praying in the Temple (Luke 18:9–14), the religious Pharisee—a moral leader in the community—has lost his soul. He is closed in on himself; his thankfulness is confined to gratitude for his own superiority. The pretense here is thrown into bold relief by the prayer of a nervous tax collector, an outcast in the community, quivering in a dark corner of the Temple. He cries to heaven, "God, be merciful to me a sinner!" It is the outcast whom God justified, concludes Jesus, for he knew both himself and God better than the Pharisee.

A similar comparison—and the same message—appears in the

tax collector Matthew's account of his own call (Matthew 9:9–13). The Pharisees criticize Jesus for eating with Matthew's friends, who are "tax collectors and sinners." Jesus replies, "Those who are well have no need of a physician, but those who are sick." The irony and sarcasm in this line is as bitter and penetrating as anything one can find in Matthew 23. The underside of a theological system that stresses judgment has always been self-righteous formalism, i.e., applying judgment to others that only externally applies to oneself. Confession or the convicting, "theological" use of the Law loses its spiritual substance and becomes an empty form. Both the cause and the consequence of this is a type of "sickness unto death," an ugly amalgam of pride and psychological masochism,[4] which is why Jesus' ironical use of medical imagery is so apt.

Since the disease is nothing to be proud of, it is usually well hidden, particularly in a religious frame where it is typically preoccupied with bringing others to health. But when encountering God's Son, the pride and lovelessness of these Pharisees comes marching out into the open, and Jesus immediately identifies it as a self-contradiction. The Pharisees pretend to obey the Law, but how can this be if they neither practice nor recognize the love that God commands? Without ever denying the particular sin of tax collectors in a period of Roman oppression, Jesus suggests that Pharisaic perfectibilism is too limited; it leaves out mercy and love of the enemy. Though kept under wraps, their spiritual pride is as great an affront to God as the extortion of tax collectors, for they do not repent. And because they do not, even tax collectors and harlots will go into the Kingdom of God before them (Matthew 21:31).

The metaphor of a counterweight scale may help here. At the heart of Christian legal piety is a precarious balance, and trouble begins the moment the balance is upset. On the one hand, Pharisaic Christians at their best are rigorously theocentric, obeying God rather than men. They combine strict obedience to God with the rebellious cry, "Non serviam," to any sovereign or institution which prohibits or compromises that obedience. This theocentrism permeates their view of the Bible, their theological temper, and their ecclesiology. At the same time, they remain acutely conscious of their moral distance from God, and of the degree to which even the most obedient Christian is caught in the vicious circle of sin and ever dependent on divine grace. The "realism" of Pharisaic Christianity reflects this second element. The connection between these two parts of the Jewish prophetic mind is illuminated nicely in the famous call of Isaiah, where in the presence of God the prophet suddenly becomes conscious that "I am a man of unclean lips, and I dwell in the midst of a people of unclean lips" (Isaiah 6:5).

It is in terms of this crucial balance that Pharisaic Christians intensify biblical law and then accommodate it so that it applies to all members of the community of faith with equal force. The balance can be upset in two ways, though usually both are present together when legal Christianity degenerates into legalism. The first imbalance could be called the *accommodationist* error, where what is lost is a sense of the beauty, the distinctiveness and the superiority of *divine* commands. The law model remains in place, however, and what is encouraged is obedience *per se*. Indiscriminate obedience to most *any* higher authority—with copious references to Romans 13 and 1 Peter 2—is promoted as morally good. The social form of this distortion is a rigid and usually corrupt conservatism; politically, it issues in a mindless type of establishmentarianism.[5]

Jesus attacked this error, and the oppressive system it generates and legitimates as well. He said simply, "You leave the commandment of God, and hold fast to the tradition of men" (Mark 7:8). This is the heart of the matter. What the error obscures is precisely the distinction between God's commands and the traditions of men. Where the capacity to make this distinction is lost, prophetic consciousness is lost also. For the genius of prophetic consciousness is to continually and accurately distinguish between divine Law, which is binding on the conscience and originates beyond time and circumstance, and human law, which is both subordinate to divine Law and contingent, i.e., changeable and the servant of expediency. Superstitious reverence for finite authorities and powers (parents, priest or presbyter, husband, employer, government and the like) has always been a mark of legalism. In Christianity, it is a parody of obedience to God, and one of its effects is to turn sensitive people away from the law model altogether.

Though rooted in a slightly different tendency, the *intensificationist* error is also a parody of true obedience. This opposite temptation in legal Christianity is to obscure what Isaiah felt so vividly in the Temple: the sense of one's own sin, and of the unity of all persons under God in tragedy and sin. When Isaiah's insight is suppressed in Pharisaic Christianity, the consequent duplicity can prompt perfectionist legalism in its ugliest form. Inordinate pride before oneself, the basic infection leading to legalism, is here allied with that pride before others typically *generated* by legalism. It is this spiritual sickness that makes the Gospels' Pharisees so offensive.

It is also what makes them dangerous. The virulence of Jesus' attack on them offers no other explanation. Their particular distortion of the Hebraic law model is not only infected by the disease of sin, making it contagious. The disease in this form carries an *ominous resistance to cure*. Behind the piety and correct exteriors of legalistic religion stalks the power of death. Jesus describes it thus: "Woe to you! for you are like graves which are not seen, and men walk over them without knowing it" (Luke 11:44). Or again: "You are like whitewashed tombs, which outwardly appear beautiful, but within are full of dead men's bones and all uncleanness" (Matthew 23:27).

The resistance to grace among Christian legalists of this type has a single, characteristic root—their perfectionist belief that the firmness of their own obedience raises them above sin with its tragic depths. "Justification" is swallowed up in "sanctification." Instead of all boasting coming to an end through faith in divine forgiveness, a religion of pride in good works continues and God is in effect proclaimed as the God of law-abiders only (Romans 3:21–31). The history of Christianity suggests that there may be no effective limit to the variety of religious masks behind which this distortion can grow. After the Reformation, Protestants demonstrated that even the doctrine of justification by faith alone is capable of being promoted in an intolerant, fanatic, and self-righteous manner![6]

Among the many damaging consequences of Christian legalism is its effect on the church. A quite proper stress on human freedom and responsibility is perverted into a shallow voluntarism; an appropriate sense of election and of the distinction between the church and the world is corrupted and becomes rigid separatism. The church's basic concern gradually turns in on itself. A stunning and original feature of Jesus' ministry—that he *sought out* sinners, strangers, the lost, even enemies—is quietly put aside, and forgotten. The work of John Calvin, perhaps the finest Christian legal mind of all time, appears to have deficiencies at this point.[7]

This is hardly the place to rehearse all the Christian biblical arguments against *their own* legalism. One does not have to be as historically skeptical about Scripture as Bultmann or Neusner to accept the fact that the New Testament writers were not controlled by the purposes of modern historiography. Their purpose everywhere is to recall Christians to faith in and obedience to God in Christ. To be sure, the controversy dialogues between Jesus and the "scribes and Pharisees" reflect both Jesus' struggle with *some* of them, and the growing conflict between the early church and its opponents. But the essential aim of the passages, to which Bultmann refers almost in passing, is to preserve an aspect of Jesus' life deemed crucial to the church's discussions within itself on questions of law.[8]

The scathing polemic against the Pharisees recorded in the Gospels is thus not an attack on the importation of the law model into Christianity, nor—properly understood—is it an attack on the Jews. Rather it is a critique of an abuse of the law model within Christianity, and stands as probably the most brilliant prophetic exposure of that diabolical temptation to which any religion with a prophetic, puritan voice is prone. Morally, it is spiritual pride. Ethically, it is allowing the law's first or "theological" use to atrophy. Theologically, it is tipping the delicate balance between law and grace toward the side of law. Christologically, it is to so absolutize works and the human knowledge of good and evil that the transcendence and mystery of God is denied even as it appears to be affirmed, and so naturally the Messiah himself is misapprehended: his teachings are squeezed into conventional categories and old wineskins; and he appears, finally and before God, just like anybody else.[9]

NOTES

1. Hans Küng, *On Being a Christian,* pp. 586–90.

2. Even scholars who appreciate the deep affinities between Jesus and the Pharisees back off from this identification. See B. Linders, "Jesus and the Pharisees," *Donum Gentilicium: New Testament Studies in Honor of David Daube,* Bammel *et al.* eds. (Oxford, 1978), pp. 51–63.

3. Robert Banks, *Jesus and the Law in the Synoptic Tradition* (London, 1975), p. 242. What is entailed in the phrase "completely transformed" is not entirely clear in the book, and perhaps cannot be. In any case, an adequate assessment of Jesus' posture on Law must eventually move beyond the evidence in the Synoptics.

4. Cf. James Gustafson, *Christ and the Moral Life,* pp. 185ff.

5. A similar distortion can be found in corrupt versions of any intellectual system with a strong predestinarian element, such as Stoicism and Calvinism.

6. Paul Tillich summarized this as the failure to submit the doctrine of justification by faith to the experience of justification by faith. Cited in Reinhold Niebuhr, *The Nature and Destiny of Man,* Vol. 2 (New York, 1943), p. 226, n. 7.

7. See Karl Barth's critique in *Church Dogmatics,* IV, 3 (Edinburgh, 1962), pp. 762–95.

8. Rudolf Bultmann, *The History of the Synoptic Tradition,* pp. 41–50.

9. Cf. Dietrich Bonhoeffer's discussion of the Pharisee as a spiritual type in his *Ethics,* pp. 26–37.

X

"THAT THEY MAY ALL BE ONE"

I do not pray for these only, but also for those who believe in
me through their word, that they may all be one; even as thou,
Father, art in me, and I in thee, that they also may be in us, so
that the world may believe that thou hast sent me.

John 17:20–21

Over twenty years ago, J. S. Whale wrote that while the love of
liberty runs deep in his own sectarian English Free Church tradition
and leaves him suspicious of the modern movement toward Christian
reunion, the liturgical barrenness and the "impenitently schismatic"
side of this same tradition convinces him that the ecumenical issue is
"the supreme issue for the Protestant tradition in this century."[1] It is
difficult to quarrel with this judgment. Though Christian divisions
are as old as Christianity, and no tradition is without responsibility
for them, the very shape of contemporary Protestantism is a distress-
ingly clear answer to Paul's famous question to the Corinthians: "Is
Christ divided?" (1 Corinthians 1:13). Isn't Phariasiac Christianity
more part of this problem than of its solution? If the thesis of this
book has any implications for the ecumenical movement, what are
they?

The ecumenical movement in our time is only the most recent in
a long series of Christian efforts to heal divisions in the church of
Christ.[2] The term "ecumenical" comes from the Greek word *oikou-
mene,* which means the inhabited earth, and points both to the global
setting of reunion efforts and to Christ's prayer that the whole world
may learn of his divinity through the unity of the universal church

with God in him (John 17). To be sure, the call to bring Christian churches into more visible unity can be little more than ecclesiastical or political centrism in religious clothing, but this need not be so. It is an imperative from Christ himself. The question is how to honor it.

The thrust of ecumenism is quite properly to realize the unity of Christians, and the movement is naturally tempted to de-emphasize the other two marks of Christ's Body (holiness, universality). This short book is a warning against *premature ecumenism,* the subordination of universality to unity when defining the church and its mission. An ecumenism which ignores or rejects Jewish Christianity is likely to be anti-semitic, and also insufficiently sensitive to Christian freedom and diversity. But the basic fault lies deeper. Such an ecumenism is a profanation of Christ in his universality, perhaps inadvertently suppressing the fact that "all things were created through him and for him" (Colossians 1:16) and that it is precisely the diversity of Christianity—canonized in the New Testament—in which the created diversity of the world is hallowed. Surely one of the messages in John 17 is that the universality of the church symbolizes the unity of the world, which suggests why premature ecumenism is so crippling: it would unify a divided church by turning away from a divided world.

The contribution of Pharisaic Christianity to the Christian view of *mission* lies here. We live in an age when the Christian global encounter with the majesty and depth of non-Christian religions has injected new meaning into the famous Isaiah passage, "My thoughts are not your thoughts, neither are my ways your ways, says the Lord" (Isaiah 55:8); and it has raised serious questions about the brash desire to "save souls."[3] The fact that decolonization in developing nations has often entailed the rejection of Christianity (e.g., China) suggests that Christian "mission" may have become too intimately tied to a Western passion for expansion and growth. In this new context, what exactly is a Christian mission meant to achieve? In Pharisaic Christianity, the church's mission is primarily to *be* something rather than to do something. It is not a special arrangement, a sales program aimed at "the heathen," but simply what the church is in a particular place, an anticipation of God's Kingdom, a witness of truth and love. The essential mission of the Christian church is not to triumph over the world, or to expand to fill it, but to reform itself and become what it is, a royal priesthood and a holy nation.[4] Pharisaic Christianity joins the Jews in one of their historic roles: challenging triumphalist views of Christian mission.

But how, then, is the church to express its universality? One way is to plant churches on indigenous foundations in every land and culture. Another is to say clearly that God alone is judge of the human conscience, and God's grace abounds, so that the boundaries around God's people should never be identified with the walls of the church. Many who appear to be outside the holy community are truly inside, and some who appear inside are actually outside.

A signal theological contribution to this search for the true universality of Christ and his Body has been the concept of "anonymous" or "latent" Christianity. Roman Catholic theologians Karl Rahner and Edward Schillebeeckx use the term "anonymous Christianity" in their work;[5] and in recent Protestant theology, Paul Tillich writes that though the Christian church is the Spiritual Community of God in explicit—albeit paradoxical—manifestation, there are also "latent Spiritual Communities" that show the power of God in an impressive way outside the organized churches. They do not belong to the church, but they are included in the Spiritual Community because some partial response to God's presence is manifest within them.[6] A difficulty with Tillich's concept is that it is undisciplined by Scripture and too vague to apply with any precision, but it points in a promising direction. Under the category of latent Spiritual Community, he includes the assembly of the people of Israel, the schools of the prophets, medieval and modern synagogues, Islamic devotional communities and mosques and theological schools, and classical mysticism in Asia and Europe.[7]

The ecumenical significance of Pharisaic Christianity should now be clearer. It marks the openness of the Christian community— the outstretched arms of Christ himself—to all those "outside" who feel drawn to a religion of the law model or to legal piety. The outstanding examples appear to be the followers of Judaism and Islam. The wider ecumenism envisaged here was represented beautifully in a statement by Pope John Paul II during his visit to Turkey in November 1979. Under pressure from Turkey's embattled Orthodox Christians to say no such thing, the Pope quoted positively from the

Koran and appealed to the world to understand the values of "the vast world of Islam." It was a remarkable speech. In one stroke he put aside the bloody history of the Crusades and stepped smartly away from the common Christian view of Islam as a fanatical religion of power and ignorance. Instead he stressed the common monotheism and geographical, spiritual ties between Islam and Christianity.[8] The Bishop of Rome was appealing here, I believe, to that unity by which all persons are attracted to Christ.

What unifies the New Testament is not a dogmatic system or an ethical code; these do not unify the world either, of course. At the center of the New Testament is a person and the Christian "gospel," the kerygmatic announcement that God meets us now as the one who was Jesus of Nazareth. It is the message that the very Kingdom of God is entering history in the form of Christ; and the surprise even today is how quietly it all happened, and how it entails the paradox that the way to victory over death's power is through trial and suffering (Mark 8:31ff; 2 Corinthians 6). God's Kingdom is a gentle Kingdom. Its outstanding marks are humility, love, patience, living for others, respect for others. In a brutal world, it is quite properly conceived as an other–worldly Kingdom, and appears destined to remain so.

Yet the salvation offered in Christ continues to be "from the Jews" (John 4:23). With Judaism, but also with Islam and Confucianism, Christianity is one of the great *this-worldly,* empire building religions. For close to two thousand years, it has had an extraordinary impact on social and political life, on reform movements, on revolutions, and on political philosophy in the West. Prompted by their faith, Christians have made alliances with a wide variety of political groups. Some of these groups are the children of a single political movement born centuries ago in Europe, and possessing deep spiritual affinities with Pharisaic Christianity. Since the late nineteenth century, it has been under attack by the thought and practice of Marxist socialism. In 1914, the strength and vitality of the movement was seriously shaken in Europe itself, and since then its history worldwide has been a story of setback and retreat. One is sorely tempted to choose from among the host of political alternatives, but they all appear to be worse.

The movement is liberalism. The *forms* of liberalism are primarily those procedural safeguards of liberty (such as the U.S. Bill of Rights) and the juridical constraints on governmental power characteristic of Western liberal democracy. Even in England which has no written constitution, the supremacy of law and of its "rule" is the institutional heart of liberalism, and is at the center of its long struggle with communism. Liberalism asserts that the first principle of politics must be liberty or respect for the personal integrity of others. This is why justice is ranked lower than liberty in liberalism: liberty is defined as moral conscience and action, and is therefore prior to and the proper arbiter of justice. In the words of the Italian liberal Benedetto Croce, when we overthrow tyranny or the oppression of outdated custom, it is to create the maximum condition of liberty in society. When we minister to the sick, it is to regain for society a source of energy, of liberty. When we educate children, it is to shape beings capable of looking after themselves freely and autonomously. When we support the just against the unjust, truth against falsehood, it is because injustice and falsehood are a surrender to passions and darkness, whereas truth and justice are acts of liberty.[9]

A typical theoretical mistake is to confuse this moral concept of liberty with a type of economic organization—either with the free market and the capitalist doctrine of economic freedom, or with the socialist ideal of economic equality. This error stems from a failure to recognize the pre-eminence of law in liberalism. The liberal concept of liberty is a "formal," juridical one: authentic liberals deny the distinction, often promoted by idealists, between formal liberty and "real" or actual liberty.[10] Many believe that though formal freedom under law has been granted to people in Western democracies, it is rendered empty by being insufficiently actualized within equitable material conditions. To the liberal mind, this is finally a distinction without a difference. Close scrutiny reveals that juridical liberty is political liberty pure and simple. There is no other kind. The other sort of "liberty" turns out to be a type of economic organization, usually the socialist organization of equality. While such an organization may have a validity for a time in given circumstances, it is not and never was the *sine qua non* of liberty.

The juridical forms of liberalism are crucial to the movement, but even more decisive is its *spirit*. Liberalism, Ortega y Gasset writes, is the supreme form of generosity. The root of the liberal ethos is the "radical progressive desire" of each individual to take others into consideration. Politically, it is the right which majorities concede to minorities; it is the system in which rulers take the noble, paradoxical, anti-natural step of limiting their power and attempting, even at their own expense, to leave room in their community for those who neither think nor feel as they do. Liberalism announces a determination to share existence with the enemy, even with an enemy that is weak. It is no accident, then, that such a refined, almost acrobatic attitude has drawn the fire of every authoritarian impulse in modern politics, particularly the wrath of probably the strongest political movement in the twentieth century—fascism. Concludes Ortega: "It is a discipline too difficult and complex to take firm root on earth."[11]

This liberal spirit is perhaps the best political elaboration not only of Jewish Christianity, but also of John 17 and ecumenical Christianity. In fact, ecumenism itself could be defined as Christian liberalism applied *intra muros*. It is the most noble, refined and fragile of existing Christian movements, imposing a difficult and complex discipline on every part of the church. And it thus should surprise no one that many churches appear anxious to get rid of it. Christians who love liberty have few higher callings today than to safeguard its forms and to inspire its spirit that will create new forms.

Without the forms of liberalism, its spirit would become vulnerable and deteriorate. This is why some belief in the procedural safeguards of freedom is necessary to protect liberty. But belief in the forms is not enough. Where free spirits are lacking, no free institution can prevail. When the spirit of liberalism weakens, the forms necessarily atrophy. Since spiritual decay is often hidden, liberals are tempted to believe that confidence in the forms of liberalism is sufficient to protect liberty. According to the Christian gospels, some Pharisees once fell into a similar trap with respect to religion and faith. The danger was real then and it is real now, for the belief that scrupulous adherence to the forms of liberalism will itself preserve liberty is probably the greatest threat to its preservation.

In sum, behind the Pharisaic Christian stress on law is the belief that the Christian church is above all a community of freedom. Over

against other institutions, its unity is more tenuous and its vulnerability to division more extreme. This is not to justify the scandal of
separatism and schism in Christianity. But it is to warn against the
oppressive burden of religion and its institutions, even when the concern is the structure of Christian unity. In the wise words of Scottish
theologian John Oman,

> I can find no sense in life and no meaning in history on the
> view that God is as much concerned with correct doctrine,
> approved action and regulated institution as man is. To
> have made us all infallible in every judgment and undeviat-
> ing in every action would surely have been child's play for
> His omnipotence. But if the sole perfect order be the free-
> dom of God's children, and it involves knowing God's
> mind of our own insight and doing His will of our own dis-
> cernment and consecration and having a relation to others
> which is a fellowship mutual both with God and man, and
> that, in the end, God will not be content with less, surely
> we can see, dimly at least, the necessity for the long hard
> way man has had to travel.[12]

"That they all may be one," prayed Jesus, "even as thou, Father, art in me, and I in thee, that they also might be in us . . ." (John
17:21). Both the proximity and the pathos of Christian unity can be
seen in this prayer, which in turn suggests the extraordinary challenge facing ecumenical Christianity. For the unity of Christ's people
is as close to us as God's rule (Kingdom) in their hearts, and any
person failing to sense this in Christian sisters and brothers has yet to
look for it. But bringing into more visible harmony the worldwide
flame of Christian freedom demands a kind of poise and defines a vocation to which many are called but perhaps few chosen. The methods of true ecumenists never violate what God himself creates in his
communion with us, which is freedom (2 Corinthians 3). This means
that the high calling of unifying Christianity has not only traveled a
"long hard way" already, but perhaps should be made a permanent
item on each church agenda, as Christians pray with their Lord
"that the world may believe that thou hast sent me" and reach

toward the day when "every knee should bow ... and every tongue confess that Jesus Christ is Lord" (Philippians 2:10–11).

NOTES

1. J. S. Whale, *The Protestant Tradition* (Cambridge, 1955), p. 225.

2. See Victor Conzemius, "Ecumenism," *Sacramentum Mundi,* Vol. 2 (New York, 1968), pp. 191–212.

3. Though the care and protection of souls appears to me to be well within the competence and calling of Christ's church, the salvation of souls is not. The church must guard against even appearing to "bring their God in their hand" (Job 12:6). In the "saving souls" approach to mission, the Pelagian overtones are so insistent that the phrase should probably be dropped.

4. Martin Honecker finds a similar view of mission in orthodox Lutheranism: "The Knowledge of God and the Limits of the 'Mission' of Christianity," *International Review of Mission* (October 1979), pp. 354–65.

5. Cited by Eugene Hillman in his suggestive book, *The Wider Ecumenism: Anonymous Christianity and the Church* (London, 1968), p. 25, *passim.*

6. Paul Tillich, *Systematic Theology,* Vol. 3 (Chicago, 1963), p. 163.

7. *Ibid.,* p. 164.

8. Cf. Walter Abbott, ed., *The Documents of Vatican II,* p. 663.

9. Benedetto Croce, *Philosophy, Poetry, History,* Sprigge tr. (London, 1966), p. 711.

10. See *Two Concepts of Liberty* (Oxford, 1958), Isaiah Berlin's classic defense of the superiority of juridical (he calls it "negative") liberty as an ideal. Even if the ideal is a late fruit of our declining capitalist civilization, he writes, even if posterity knows and honors it as little as did primitive societies, "principles are not less sacred because their duration cannot be guaranteed. Indeed, the very desire for guarantees that our values are eternal and secure in some objective heaven is perhaps only a craving for the certainties of childhood or the absolute values of our primitive past. 'To realize the relative validity of one's convictions,' said an admirable writer of our time, 'and yet stand for them unflinchingly, is what distinguishes a civilized man from a barbarian.' To demand more than this is perhaps a deep and incurable metaphysical need; but to allow it to guide one's practice is a symptom of an equally deep, and far more dangerous, moral and political immaturity" (p. 57).

11. José Ortega y Gasset, *The Revolt of the Masses* (New York, 1932), p. 76.

12. John Oman, *Honest Religion* (Cambridge, 1941), p. 169.

EPILOGUE

Eternal peace have those
   who love thy law;
   and nothing shall offend them.
Psalm 119:165 (KJV)

Every view of the world has an inner life of its own, a life to which influences and reactions are secondary. At the center of each philosophy, much as a spider who has spun an elaborate web, sits a living philosopher. However, the philosopher is usually difficult to see, because again like a spider he prefers to remain out of sight and leave the web with an appearance of having spun itself. The motive here is not often modesty, but rather embarrassment about a most potent factor in the creation of theories: temperament.

A philosopher of pragmatism and an astute observer of human nature, William James wrote that the entire history of philosophy

> is to a great extent that of a certain clash of human temperaments. . . . Of whatever temperament a professional philosopher is, he tries, when philosophizing, to sink the fact of his temperament. Temperament is no conventionally recognized reason, so he urges impersonal reasons for his conclusions. Yet his temperament really gives him a stronger bias than any of his more objective premises. . . . He *trusts* his temperament.[1]

What James said of philosophy can be applied to theology, to biblical interpretation, to ethics, and in particular to this book. "Eternal peace have those who love thy law," reads the psalm, but the psalm does not say there is no other way to obtain peace. This book not

128

only proposes a somewhat angular moral position; it is addressed by and to a certain sort of person.

To whom exactly is this book addressed? It is aimed at the deontological mind. The book is designed for those people who find the law model appealing, and are attracted to its distinctive moral quest. To be sure, these people are historical beings with widely varying outlooks, reflecting their particular circumstances and culture; their capacity to apprehend the Law is in diverse ways clouded; their interpretations are always subject to rationalization. But however obscured and distorted, at the very center of their being each is aware of a peculiar claim. The moral meaning of this claim is categorical and absolute, even though it comes to them through a veritable fog of inconsistencies and relativities. To such a person, the task of morality is to clarify this standard, to justify and elaborate it in a particular time and place. Obedience to it is understood to belong to the essential dignity of man. He can no more escape from it than from his own reality.[2]

The book is also an explicitly political appeal. Pharisaic Christianity is liberal self-criticism from the right, and is aimed at Christians who are disturbed at the drift away from biblical authority in the political pronouncements characteristic of much Christian liberalism. In addition, it is meant to encourage Christians resisting the conservative transmutation of biblical law into an ideology opposing equality, freedom, and helping the weak.

It is a political appeal as well to those who find themselves at once stimulated by the thought of Karl Marx and troubled by the Christian alliance with Marxism, particularly by its moral consequences. The alliance is explicit today in liberation theology, the most aggressive and politically insightful of current theologies. Given the cataclysmic revolutions and gods that have failed in the past sixty years, this is a subject about which it is difficult to remain neutral. Marx's ingenious critique of capitalism and of the Christian religion has permanent importance, and it is certainly no mistake to see in his work the bracing compassion of the Hebrew prophets. But the confusions and political dangers of Marxism outweigh its value. No one is helped by leftist proposals which proceed as if Sir Karl Popper, Michael Polanyi, Reinhold Niebuhr, Bernard-Henri Lévy, and Alexander Solzhenitsyn never wrote a word. The propensities to self-deception and violence in Marxist systems are massive; there are better ways for Christians to move into politics.

But in one sense, hopefully, this book is for everyone. With its view of life as a political system and with its legal piety, Pharisaic Christianity in its own way points beyond itself to what some ethicists like to call "the moral"—the universal human quest for the right and the good. The quest is unique, for it involves judging behavior in a completely distinctive way. To call a particular course of action healthy, or logical, or reactionary, or impolite, or fun, or painful, or successful, or (yes, even) legal is to make some interesting and important claims, but not one of them tells us anything necessarily about whether the action is right or wrong, good or bad.[3] Moral judgment is a very special kind of judgment, and is absolutely inescapable. The search for a moral position one can hold with integrity is one of the supremely critical questions in human life. The only detour I know is through a determinist denial of man's moral nature and free will, which is in the end always some form of "looking the other way" and of bad faith. The moral quest is everybody's quest, and if the book lures readers—whatever their temperament—into even a small advance, the web of this little spider will have done its job.

NOTES

1. William James, *Pragmatism* (New York, 1907), pp. 6–7.
2. Some of this paragraph is derived from a most dependable deontological mind, N. H. G. Robinson, *The Groundwork of Christian Ethics* (London, 1971), pp. 43–44.
3. Henry Stob, *Ethical Reflections* (Grand Rapids, 1978), pp. 17–20.